INVESTIGA *for* GCSE Biology

Teacher's Book

P W Freeland

BSc MPhil DipEd FIBiol
Head of Science, Worth School, Sussex

HODDER AND STOUGHTON
LONDON SYDNEY AUCKLAND TORONTO

Acknowledgment

I would like to express thanks to Mrs M Moore, laboratory assistant, for preparing materials for these investigations, and to my pupils, both past and present, for their part in obtaining results.

Freeland, P.W.
    Investigations for GCSE biology.
    Teachers book
    1. Biology—Experiments
    I. Title
    574'.0724   QH316.5

    ISBN 0 340 40526 0

First published 1987
Second impression 1987

Copyright © 1987 P W Freeland

All rights reserved. No part of this publication may be reproduced or transmitted in any form or by any means, electronic or mechanical, including photocopy, recording, or any information storage and retrieval system, without permission in writing from the publisher or under licence from the Copyright Licensing Agency Limited. Further details of such licences (for reprographic reproduction) may be obtained from the Copyright Licensing Agency Limited, of 7 Ridgemount street, London WC1E 7AE

Set by Macmillan India Ltd, Bangalore 25
Printed in Great Britain
for Hodder and Stoughton Educational
a division of Hodder and Stoughton Ltd, Mill Road
Dunton Green, Sevenoaks, Kent by Page Bros (Norwich) Ltd.

Preface

Investigations for GCSE Biology is written for pupils in the 14–16 age range. It contains a collection of practical investigations suitable for GCSE examination courses in biology. The introduction of these syllabuses has provided an opportunity for a change in direction and emphasis. Extensive practical investigation at this level is an imaginative step, demanding practice and testing in a number of skills. A sound training in these skills is essential if pupils are to understand the nature of scientific investigation. Equally important is the need to present biology as a useful science, with technological and economic implications. In order to make this point, a large amount of novel material has been included. Written to link the theoretical content of GCSE syllabuses to new, imaginative, science-based practical work, the book is aimed at the top 60 per cent of the ability range.

Each investigation is introduced by a brief statement of background information and a list of materials. This may be followed by a period of preparation, in which pupils set up apparatus, and one of observation, in which they make readings and record data. Each investigation concludes with a period of questioning in which a pupil's understanding of the task is assessed. The investigations, occupying between 30 and 90 minutes, are each scored against a 20-point marking scheme. Most of the investigations test several different practical skills, listed on page (iv) of the teacher's guide. An attempt has been made to include tasks with different degrees of difficulty. Teachers may therefore base their marking on parts of investigations, adapting material to meet the needs of their classes. Approximate times required for preparation, observation, and investigation are given. At the end of each assessment, proposals for further work are listed. For example, pupils may be asked to design experiments. They must list their materials, write out their method, and draw tables, with headings, for their results. Alternatively, they may be asked to formulate hypotheses, design a method for testing them, and predict the outcomes if the hypotheses are correct.

Teaching for pupil success should be the main aim. Purposeful control, combined with a sympathetic, encouraging approach, creates a good atmosphere for carrying out investigations. Pupils should fully understand their instructions before they attempt any investigation. Safety precautions may need to be explained and discussed before they are put into effect. Skills must be practised, and rehearsed, before they are assessed. Indeed, rehearsal is often to be encouraged. Even if pupils are thoroughly familiar with the tasks they are required to carry out, it is still possible to put them into rank order on the basis of individual performance.

The teacher's guide lists skills tested in each investigation, and provides instructions and notes for teachers and laboratory assistants. Materials required for each investigation are listed. Addresses of suppliers of unfamiliar materials are also provided. The results published in this book are those obtained by pupils, working under the author's supervision; no claims are made as to their accuracy.

P.W.F.

Contents

Skills tested in the investigations	vi
1 Drawing specimens	1
2 Making and using keys	3
3 Testing for reducing sugars	4
4 Reducing sugars, starch and proteins in foods	7
5 Estimation of vitamin C	8
6 Sugar and salt in food	10
7 Spoilage of food by micro-organisms	12
8 The souring of milk	14
9 Environmental conditions affecting the digestion of starch	16
10 The effect of different temperatures on trypsin activity	18
11 Measuring enzyme activity by gas production	20
12 Using enzymes to extract fruit juice: an introduction to biotechnology	22
13 Enzyme inhibition by drugs	24
14 Sugar, bacteria and tooth decay	26
15 Demonstrating and making use of diffusion	28
16 Diffusion of water through natural and artificial membranes	30
17 Water loss from leaves	32
18 Osmosis in living tissue	34
19 Using a simple potometer	36
20 Factors affecting the rate of photosynthesis	38
21 Gas production by Canadian pondweed during photosynthesis	41
22 Visits by bees to flowers	43
23 Floral structure of tulip and polyanthus	45
24 Wind as an agent of pollination and seed dispersal	47
25 Distribution of seeds around a tree	49
26 Depth of sowing and its effects on germination	51

27	Producing new plants from stem cuttings	54
28	Comparing rates of growth in parts of a seedling	56
29	Tropic responses and auxin production	59
30	Differences between seeds and seedlings	60
31	Adaptation: form and function in plant stems	63
32	Behaviour of the woodlouse	65
33	Body size in mammals	67
34	Exercise: measuring performance	69
35	Carbon dioxide in inspired and expired air	71
36	Fermentation of glucose by yeast	73
37	Making use of yeast	75
38	The effects of a selective weedkiller on a lawn	77
39	The effects of artificial fertiliser on a population of water plants	79
40	Some characteristics of a population of trees	81
41	Finding the size of an animal population	83
42	Pollution of water and air	85
43	Organic pollution of water samples	88
44	Water retention by sand, loam and peat soils	90
45	Soil pH	92
46	Organic matter in soil	94
47	Decomposers in the soil	96
48	Gene recombination	97
49	The sense of taste	99
50	The skin as a sense organ	101
Further reading		102
Index		103
Names and addresses of suppliers		104

Skills tested in the investigations

Practical skills and processes

Observing

1 Presenting observations as drawings
2 Making scale drawings
3 Observing similarities and/or differences between specimens
4 Observing animal behaviour
5 Offering simple explanations for observations

Investigating

6 Following instructions accurately
7 Measuring accurately and systematically
8 Manipulating apparatus
9 Designing an experiment
10 Selecting apparatus for an experiment
11 Criticising the design of an experiment
12 Improving the design of an experiment
13 Tabulating results
14 Expressing results in the form of a graph
15 Performing calculations

Interpreting

16 Making deductions from the results of experiments
17 Comparing results from different experiments
18 Formulating hypotheses
19 Testing hypotheses
20 Predicting the outcome of tests if hypotheses are (a) correct, or (b) incorrect

Special skills, knowledge and understanding

21 Making artificial keys for the identification of organisms, etc.
22 Maintaining a living population of organisms
23 Making field studies of organisms
24 Understanding the principles of Mendelian inheritance
25 Understanding and applying evolutionary principles

Skill

Investigation	1	2	3	4	5	6	7	8	9	10	11	12	13	14	15	16	17	18	19	20	21	22	23	24	25
1	√	√	√																						
2			√																		√				
3					√	√	√	√					√	√		√									
4					√	√	√	√					√			√									
5					√	√	√	√							√	√									
6					√	√	√	√					√	√	√	√	√								
7	√				√	√		√	√										√						
8			√		√	√	√	√					√	√	√										
9					√	√	√	√					√	√	√										
10					√	√	√	√	√	√	√	√	√	√	√	√									
11					√	√	√	√	√	√	√	√	√	√											
12					√	√	√	√	√	√	√	√	√	√	√	√									
13					√	√	√	√	√	√	√	√	√		√										
14					√	√			√	√			√					√	√	√					
15					√	√	√	√	√				√	√	√	√									
16					√	√	√	√					√	√	√	√									
17					√	√	√	√					√		√	√	√								
18					√	√	√	√			√	√	√	√	√	√									
19					√	√	√	√					√	√	√	√									
20					√	√	√	√	√	√			√	√	√										
21					√	√	√	√	√	√			√	√											
22				√	√	√	√						√	√		√		√					√		
23	√		√		√	√																			
24	√	√	√		√	√							√	√											
25					√	√	√						√	√	√	√							√		
26					√	√	√	√					√			√		√							
27					√	√						√				√									
28					√	√	√	√				√				√									
29					√	√	√	√								√									
30	√	√	√		√	√										√									
31	√		√		√	√																			√
32				√	√	√			√																
33					√	√	√	√					√	√		√		√							
34					√	√	√		√	√			√	√	√	√									
35					√	√	√	√					√		√	√		√		√					
36					√	√	√						√	√	√	√									
37					√	√	√	√					√	√	√	√			√						
38					√	√	√	√				√	√		√	√							√		
39					√	√	√	√					√									√			
40					√	√	√	√			√	√	√	√	√	√		√					√		
41				√	√	√	√	√					√		√	√		√					√		
42					√	√	√	√					√	√	√	√			√						
43					√	√	√	√	√	√			√	√	√	√						√			
44					√	√	√	√			√	√	√	√	√										
45					√	√	√	√					√	√	√										
46					√	√	√	√			√	√	√		√	√		√		√					
47					√	√	√	√				√	√	√	√	√		√					√		
48						√							√		√									√	
49					√	√	√						√		√			√	√						
50					√	√				√					√			√	√						

1 Drawing specimens

TIME
Investigation: 30–40 minutes
April–October

Skills tested: 1, 2, 3.

Materials

- Pear ▪ Leaf of horse chestnut ▪ Preserved locust ▪ Scissors
- Forceps ▪ Hand lens ▪ Ruler, graduated in millimetres

Instructions and notes

1 The pear, horse-chestnut leaf and locust form a group of specimens with different levels of structural complexity. In order to test pupils' ability to draw specimens, any similar group of specimens could be provided.

Answers

Part A   Marks

1 See Figure 1.   4

Fig. 1 *Pear*

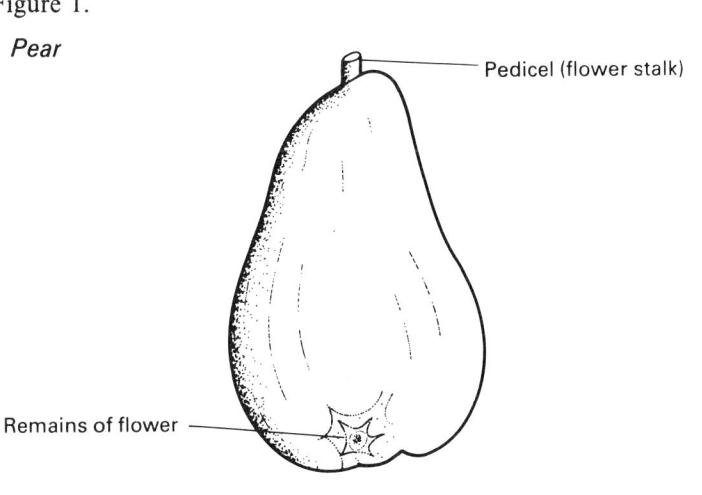

(Pedicel (flower stalk); Remains of flower)

Part B

2 See Figure 2. 6

Fig. 2 *Leaf of horse chestnut*

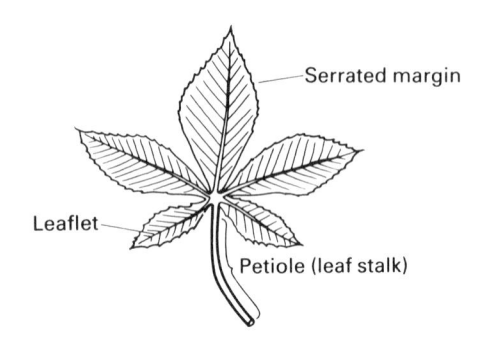

Part C

3 See Figure 3. 10

Fig. 3 *Ventral view of a locust*

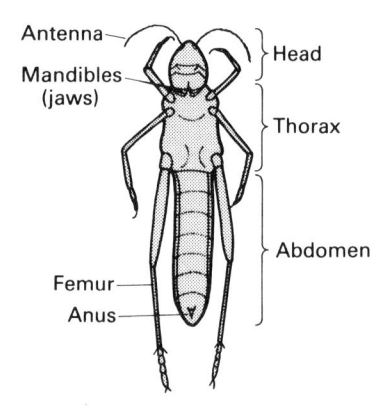

Award: (i) one mark for each drawing made to the correct scale;
(ii) one mark for each correctly labelled feature;
(iii) additional marks for the overall accuracy and quality of the drawing.

2 Making and using keys

TIME
Investigation: 30–40 minutes

Skills tested: 3, 21.

Materials

- 2 p, 5 p and 10 p coins ■ Preserved locust, labelled A ■ Defrosted complete prawn, labelled B ■ Leaf of horse chestnut, labelled C ■ Leaf of hazel, labelled D ■ Ruler, graduated in millimetres

Instructions and notes

1 Complete frozen prawns (not peeled prawns), available from supermarkets and fishmongers, should be kept at room temperature for 2–3 hours before they are given to pupils.
2 Any compound, palmate leaf may be used in place of horse chestnut, and any simple, ovate leaf, with a pointed apex, may be used in place of hazel. As venation in hazel is variable, only those leaves with obvious alternate venation should be used.

Answers

Part A   Marks

1 (a) Metal coin; 'copper' coin; about 3 cm diameter, with plumed feather design.   2
   (b) Metal coin; 'silver' coin; about 2 cm diameter, with crown-and-thistle design.   2
   (c) Metal coin; 'silver' coin; about 3 cm diameter, with rose-and-thistle design.   2

Part B

2 (a) Insects.   1
   (b) Bilaterally symmetrical; body segmented; body covered by an exoskeleton; one pair of antennae; three pairs of legs.   2
   (c) Crustaceans.   1
   (d) Bilaterally symmetrical; body segmented; body covered by an exoskeleton; two pairs of antennae.   2

Part C

3	1	Leaf simple	2
		Leaf compound	6
	2	Leaf linear, parallel veined	H
		Leaf net veined	3
	3	Leaf lobed	4
		Leaf ovate	5
	4	Leaf with rounded apex, opposite veins, six lobes	F
		Leaf with pointed apex, veins arising from a single point, five lobes	G
	5	Leaf with alternate veins, pointed apex	D
		Leaf with opposite veins, rounded apex	E
	6	Leaf palmate	C
		Leaf pinnate	I 8

3 Testing for reducing sugars

TIME
Investigation: 40–50 minutes

Skills tested: 5, 6, 7, 8, 13, 14, 16.

Materials

■ Sugars A, B, C and D ■ Cubes of potato (X), onion (Y) and apple (Z) ■ Four boiling tubes in a rack ■ 20 cm^3 sucrose solution ■ 1 cm^3 dilute hydrochloric acid ■ 1 cm^3 invertase concentrate (2) ■ Benedict's solution ■ Six Clinistix reagent strips (4, 5) ■ Eight Clinitest tablets (4, 5) ■ Clinitest colour chart ■ Two 1 cm^3 plastic syringes ■ 10 cm^3 plastic syringe ■ Ten flat-bottomed tubes ■ Test tube holder ■ Forceps ■ Spatula ■ Bunsen burner ■ Glass-marking pen ■ Safety spectacles ■ Plastic gloves ■ Graph paper

Instructions and notes

1 Benedict's solution, or reagent
  This may be prepared from the following compounds:
  7.3 g sodium citrate
  10.0 g anhydrous sodium carbonate in 80 cm^3 water
  Add to 1.7 g copper (II) sulphate in 20 cm^3 water.
2 The sucrose solution contains 4 g sucrose dissolved in 100 cm^3 water.

3 Each pupil will require approximately 0.5 g of each of the following sugars:
   A – glucose   C – fructose
   B – sucrose   D – maltose
   Samples should be crushed in a mortar to obscure their identity, and supplied wrapped in small pieces of filter paper. These may be lettered with a pencil.

> **Clinitest tablets contain concentrated sodium hydroxide. Pupils should wear safety spectacles and plastic gloves when handling this reagent, and when heating Benedict's solution. When cubes of tissue are boiled in Benedict's solution, 'bumping' may occur, causing hot, alkaline liquid to spill from the boiling tubes. This may be prevented by gently moving the base of the boiling tube from side to side while it is heating, or by adding a few small, glass beads or pebbles to the mixture.**

4 Cubes of potato (X), onion (Y) and apple (Z), each approximately 1 cm^3, may be supplied in a labelled petri dish. Amounts of reducing sugars present will depend on (i) the varieties used, and (ii) the time of year at which the investigation is carried out.

5 As an economy measure, each Clinistix reagent strip may be cut longitudinally into two pieces.

Answers

Part A   Marks

2 (a) See Table 1.   4

Table 1

Sugar	Benedict's test (✓ or ✗)
A	✓
B	✗
C	✓
D	✓

  (b) Sugar B.   1
  (c) Sugar B is non-reducing.   1
  (d) Boil sugar B with dilute hydrochloric acid, then test the resulting
      mixture by boiling it with Benedict's solution.   2

Part B
3 See Table 2. 4

Table 2

Plant material	Mass glucose (g) per 100 cm³ tissue sap
Potato (X)	0.75 (or more)
Onion (Y)	0.25
Apple (Z)	0.75 (or more)

Part C
5 (a) See Figures 4 and 5. 6
   (b) At room temperature, both hydrochloric acid and invertase cause sucrose to be hydrolysed to reducing sugars. The rate at which reducing sugars formed was more rapid with invertase than with hydrochloric acid. 2

Fig. 4 *Production of reducing sugar in the presence of hydrochloric acid*

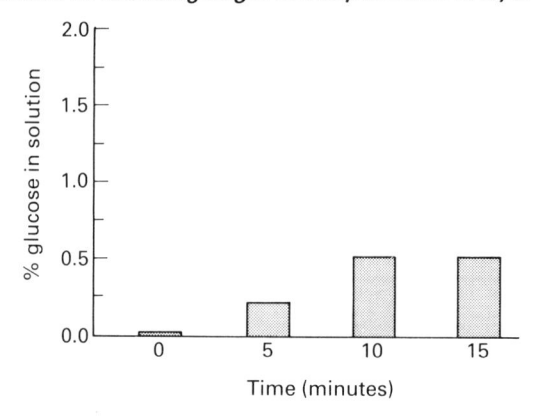

[Bar chart: % glucose in solution vs Time (minutes). Bars at 0: ~0.0; 5: ~0.2; 10: ~0.5; 15: ~0.5]

Fig. 5 *Production of reducing sugar in the presence of invertase*

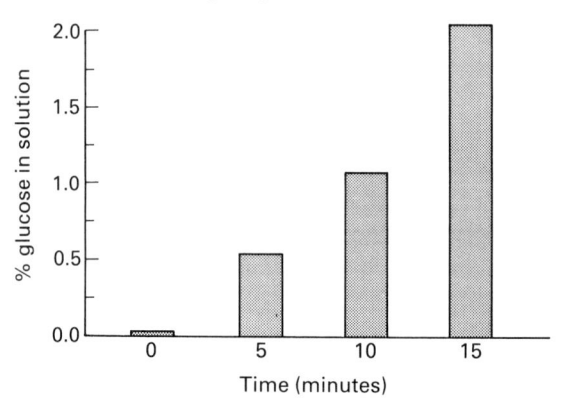

[Bar chart: % glucose in solution vs Time (minutes). Bars at 0: ~0.0; 5: ~0.5; 10: ~1.0; 15: ~2.0]

4 Reducing sugars, starch and proteins in foods

TIME
Investigation: 30–40 minutes

Skills tested: 5, 6, 7, 13, 16.

Materials

- Six Clinistix reagent strips (4, 5) ■ Five Albustix reagent strips (4, 5) ■ Iodine solution, in a dropping bottle ■ 100 cm^3 beaker of tap water ■ Two portions of white bread (each approximately 2 cm^3) ■ Slice of banana ■ Slice of cucumber ■ Portion of cheddar cheese (approximately 1 cm^3) ■ Two soaked raisins/sultanas ■ White tile ■ Scalpel

Instructions and notes

1. The solution of iodine may be prepared by dissolving 4 g potassium iodide and 2 g iodine in 1 dm^3 water.
2. The raisins/sultanas should be soaked in water for 24 hours before they are distributed.
3. All of the foodstuffs may be distributed to pupils in a single container, such as a petri dish, sub-divided into five segments by ink markings.
4. In order to reduce costs, each Clinistix and Albustix reagent strip may be cut longitudinally into two halves. These reagents should be supplied in separate, stoppered, flat-bottomed tubes.

Answers

		Marks
1	See Table 3.	15
2	(a) Banana and raisin/sultana produced similar colour changes.	1
	(b) Cucumber and cheese produced similar colour changes.	1
	(c) White bread.	1
3	(a) Maltose.	1
	(b) Amylase in saliva has catalysed the breakdown of starch into maltose.	1

7

Table 3

Test	Foodstuff	Colour change in Clinistix (reducing sugars)	Colour change in Albustix (protein)	Starch test (starch)
(a)	White bread	absent	present	present
(b)	Banana	present	present	present
(c)	Cucumber	present	present	absent
(d)	Cheese	absent	present	absent
(e)	Raisin/sultana	present	present	absent

5 Estimation of vitamin C

TIME
Investigation: 40–60 minutes

Skills tested: 5, 6, 7, 8, 15, 16.

Materials

- 50 mg vitamin C tablet, labelled A ■ 25 mg vitamin C tablet, labelled B ■ Four DCPIP tablets (2) ■ 15 cm^3 grapefruit juice ■ 1 g sodium hydrogen carbonate (bicarbonate) ■ 150 cm^3 water in beaker ■ Two pestles and mortars (one exclusively for the DCPIP solution) ■ Two 100 cm^3 beakers (with a 50^3 cm graduation) ■ 10 cm^3 plastic syringe ■ 1 cm^3 plastic syringe ■ Boiling tube in a test-tube rack ■ Litmus paper ■ Test-tube holder ■ Bunsen burner ■ Forceps ■ Wash-bottle, containing distilled water ■ Glass beads ■ Glass rod ■ Knife ■ Safety spectacles

Instructions and notes

1. Tablets containing 25 mg and 50 mg vitamin C are available from pharmacists.
2. Grapefruit juice may be obtained from ripe fruit, or a carton of fresh juice may be purchased from a supermarket.

> **When grapefruit juice is heated over a bunsen burner, precautions should be taken to prevent 'bumping'. Before the juice is heated, 2–3 glass beads should be added. Gentle heat should be applied to raise the temperature to the boiling point.**

3. Each pupil with require access to a sink with a cold tap.
4. This investigation is intended for more able pupils.

Answers

	Marks

4. (a) Volume of vitamin C solution A = 0.8–1.2 cm³ — 2
   (b) Vitamin C content of tablet (mg)

$$= \frac{\text{volume (cm}^3\text{) solution containing tablet}}{\text{volume (cm}^3\text{) solution containing 1 mg vitamin C}}$$

$$= \frac{50}{1} = 50 \text{ mg} \qquad 3$$

5. (a) Volume of vitamin C solution B = 1.8–2.2 cm³ — 2
   (b) $\frac{50}{2} = 25$ mg — 3

6. (a) Volume of grapefruit juice = 1.3–2.2 cm³ (depending on source) — 1
   (b) $\frac{100}{1.8} = 55.5$ mg vitamin C/100 cm³ juice (typical result) — 1

7. (a) Red — 1
   (b) Grapefruit juice is acid. — 1

8. (a) Bubbles of gas/effervescence/frothing — 1
   (b) The acid in grapefruit juice reacted with bicarbonate, releasing carbon dioxide. — 1
   (c) Volume boiled grapefruit juice = 3.0–6.0 cm³ — 1
   (d) $\frac{100}{5.0} = 20$ mg vitamin C/100 cm³ juice (typical result) — 1
   (e) The vitamin C content was reduced. — 1

9. Some vitamin C in the beans would be destroyed. — 1

6 Sugar and salt in food

TIME
Investigation: 50–60 minutes

Skills tested: 5, 6, 7, 8, 13, 14, 15, 16, 17.

Materials

■ 25 cm³ glucose solution ■ 25 cm³ distilled water ■ 11 cm³ orange squash ■ 11 cm³ concentrated orange juice ■ 10 cm³ plastic syringe ■ Four flat-bottomed tubes, approximately 8 × 2 cm ■ Four strips of blotting paper, each 1 × 10 cm ■ Ruler, graduated in millimetres ■ Top-pan balance ■ Glass-marking pen ■ Graph paper

Instructions and notes

1 The glucose solution is prepared by dissolving 10 g glucose in 50 cm³ water, and adding water to make the volume up to 100 cm³.
2 Cut four similar strips of blotting paper, with parallel sides, for each pupil. Thick blotting paper gives the best results.
3 This investigation is suited to more able pupils working in small groups.

Answers

Part A   **Marks**

4 See Table 4.   2

Table 4

Mixture number	1	2	3	4
Volume glucose solution in syringe (cm³)	0.0	2.5	5.0	10.0
Volume water in syringe (cm³)	10.0	7.5	5.0	0.0
Mass of water or solution + syringe (g)	25.9	26.0	26.2	26.4
Mass of syringe (g)	15.9	15.9	15.9	15.9
Mass of sol'n or water (g)	10.0	10.1	10.3	10.5

5 See Figure 6. 6

Fig. 6 *Relationship between the glucose content of a solution and the mass of 10 cm³*

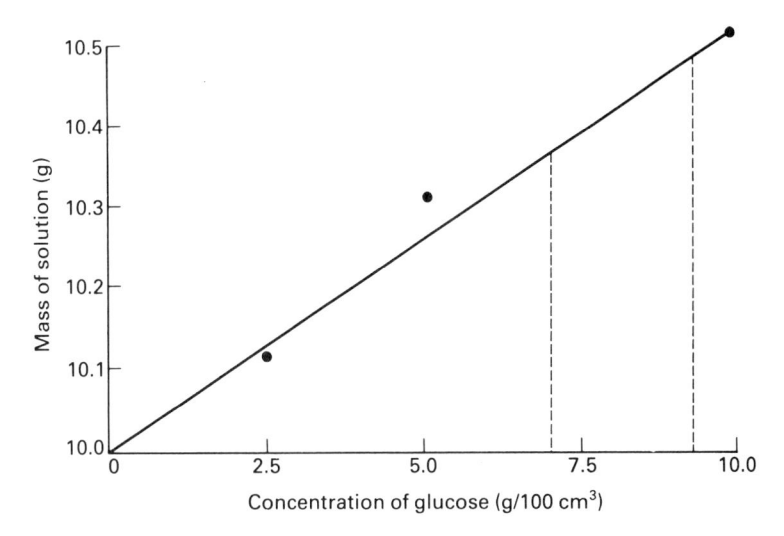

[Graph: Mass of solution (g) vs Concentration of glucose (g/100 cm³), showing a linear relationship with data points plotted and dashed lines at approximately 7.0 and 8.5 g/100 cm³]

6 (a) 10.45 g   1
  (b) 10.35 g   1

7 (a) Mass = 10.5 g = 10 g glucose/100 cm³   2
  (b) Mass = 10.4 g = 8.5 g glucose/100 cm³   2

Part B

8 (a) See Table 5

Table 5

Concentration of glucose (g/100 cm³)	0.0	2.5	5.0	10.0
Length of wet paper (cm)	4.8	4.6	4.0	3.4

   (b) The greater the distance over which water diffuses, the more dilute is the solution (or the shorter the distance, the greater the concentration). 1

9 Recording mass is a quantitative method, but difficult to use because increasing amounts of glucose cause only small increases in mass. Using strips of blotting paper is a simpler method, but one that does not always produce reliable results, as the paper may collapse. 2

11

7 Spoilage of food by micro-organisms

TIME
Preparation: 15–20 minutes
Investigation: 30–40 minutes

Skills tested: 1, 5, 6, 8, 9, 19.

Materials

Preparation

■ Banana, peach or orange ■ Potato ■ Plate of nutrient agar (or malt agar) ■ Three test tubes in a rack ■ 1 g sodium chloride ■ 5 cm^3 plastic syringe ■ Bunsen burner ■ Incubator, maintained at 35°C ■ Test tube holder ■ Ruler, graduated in millimetres ■ Scalpel ■ Cotton wool ■ Glass-marking pen ■ Safety spectacles

Investigation

■ Plate of nutrient agar (or malt agar), with colonies of microorganisms ■ Banana, peach or orange, with bruises and cuts ■ Test tubes, containing cubes of potato

Instructions and notes

1 To prepare the nutrient agar, mix 2.5 g nutrient agar powder with a little cold water to form a slurry. Add this to 100 cm^3 boiling water. Alternatively, mix 2 g agar powder and a teaspoon of malt extract with a little cold water, and add this to 100 cm^3 boiling water, stirring until the mixture is evenly distributed.

> *Plates of agar containing colonies of bacteria and fungi should be sealed with adhesive tape before they are presented to pupils. Similarly, any fruits heavily contaminated with fungal spores should be placed inside sealed polythene bags. At the end of the investigation all material containing micro-organisms should be collected, placed in a heat-resistant plastic bag, and incinerated.*

See Figure 7.

Fig. 7 *Sealing a petri dish with adhesive tape*

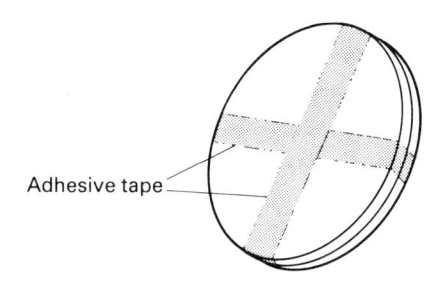

2 The investigation may be carried out 3–5 days after materials have been prepared, depending on the rate at which micro-organisms grow on the agar plates and damaged fruits. In order to present material in a suitable condition, it may be necessary to transfer some petri dishes and fruits to an incubator maintained above 35°C, or to a refrigerator.

Answers

	Marks
1 (a) See Figure 8	2

Fig. 8 *Appearance of the agar plate*

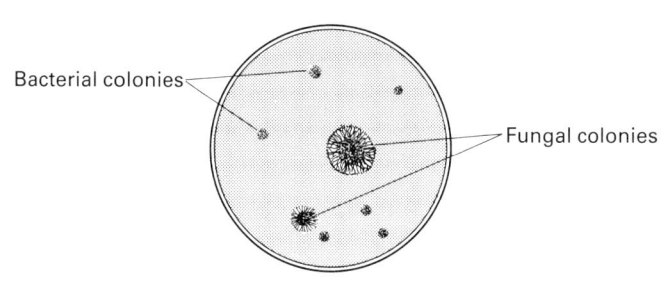

    (b) Colonies of bacteria are small, round and creamy in texture. They may be white, red, brown, or transparent. Colonies of fungi are larger and are black, grey, or brown. They consist of thread-like strands (hyphae), resembling fibres of cotton wool.   2

2 Bacteria and fungi will also grow on food intended for human consumption if it is left exposed to the air. As some of these bacteria and fungi may cause diseases, food should always be covered.   2

3 (a) (i) The bruised part darkened, and became 'watery', possibly as a result of the growth of bacteria.   1

      (ii) Fungi grew over some parts of the cut surface.   1

    (b) Fruit is more likely to be attacked by micro-organisms if it is damaged either by bruising or cutting.   2

4 (a) The liquid is cloudy. Bacteria have grown in the water surrounding the potato. 2
   (b) The liquid is clear. Boiling has killed any micro-organisms in the tube. The plug of cotton wool has prevented other micro-organisms in the air from entering. 2
   (c) The liquid is clear. Salt has acted as a preservative, preventing the growth of bacteria and fungi. 2
5 Crush the skin of an orange to a pulp. Dip a piece of filter paper into the pulp. Prepare an agar plate and leave it exposed to air for 5–10 minutes. Place the dipped filter paper on the plate. Incubate the plate. If the compound kills bacteria and fungi, none will grow on the agar immediately surrounding the filter paper. 4

8 The souring of milk

TIME
Preparation: 5 minutes per day for 7 days
Investigation: 40–50 minutes

Skills tested: 3, 5, 6, 7, 8, 13, 14, 15, 16.

Materials

Preparation

- Seven 100 cm^3 beakers or paper cups ■ Fresh milk (required daily for 7 days) ■ Glass-marking pen.

Investigation

- Seven samples of milk, numbered 1–7 ■ Narrow range pH 4.0–7.0 indicator papers (2) ■ 50 cm^3 resazurin solution (2) ■ Seven flat-bottomed tubes ■ 5 cm^3 plastic syringe ■ Forceps ■ Ruler, graduated in millimetres ■ Glass-marking pen ■ Graph paper

Instructions and notes

1 The resazurin solution is prepared from tablets. Dissolve 1 tablet in 50 cm^3 distilled water. Solutions of resazurin must be freshly made on the day they are required.

Answers

Part A
Marks

1. Milk sample 1 has thickened, or solidified, while milk sample 7 is liquid.   2
Milk sample 1 has a strong, unpleasant odour. Milk sample 7 is odourless.   2
2. See Table 6.   4

Table 6

Milk sample No.	1	2	3	4	5	6	7
pH	4.0	4.0	4.4	4.7	5.3	5.9	6.5

3. See Figure 9   4

Fig. 9 *Changes in pH during the souring of milk*

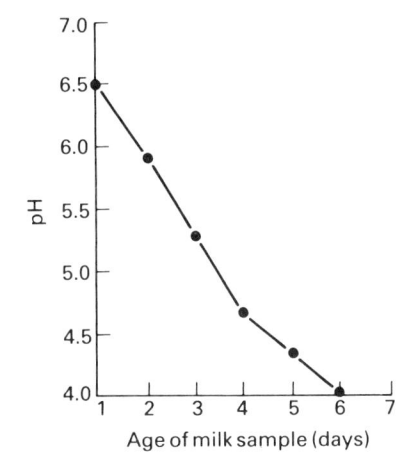

[Graph showing pH on y-axis (4.0 to 7.0) versus Age of milk sample (days) on x-axis (1 to 7), with a decreasing curve from about 6.5 at day 1 down to 4.0 at day 6-7.]

4. $\dfrac{4.0 + 4.0 + 4.4 + 4.7 + 5.3 + 5.9 + 6.5}{7} = 4.97$ 2

Part B

6. See Table 7.   2

Table 7

Tube No.	1	2	3	4	5	6	7
Colour of mixture	Pink	Pink	Pink	Pink	Pink	Blue	Blue

7 The pink colour faded, but the blue colour persisted.
8 Resazurin provides a rapid test for the souring of milk. It acts as a pH indicator, producing a blue colour with fresh milk (pH > 5.8), but a pink colour with soured milk (pH < 5.8). Additionally, it is reduced to a colourless compound by living bacteria. The pink colour fades if bacteria are present in the sample. Dairies use the dye to show that their milk is fresh.

9 Environmental conditions affecting the digestion of starch

TIME

Investigation: 40–50 minutes

Skills tested: 5, 6, 7, 8, 13, 16.

Materials

- Four test tubes, each containing 5 cm³ starch suspension, in a rack
- 10 cm³ solution X
- 5 cm³ solution Y
- Iodine solution
- 250 cm³ beaker, containing ice
- 250 cm³ beaker
- Three 5 cm³ plastic syringes
- Four glass rods
- Four plastic straws
- White tile
- Stop-clock, or watch with a second hand
- Bunsen burner
- Tripod and gauze
- Thermometer
- Paper towel
- Glass-marking pen

Instructions and notes

1 The suspension of starch is prepared by mixing 15 g soluble starch powder to a thin paste with 50 cm³ water. This is added to 1 dm³ boiling water and stirred. Allow the suspension to cool to room temperature before it is distributed.
2 Solutions X and Y are prepared by dissolving 1 g crude pancreatic amylase in 100 cm³ water. Solution Y is then boiled for 1 minute and cooled to room temperature.
3 A bench solution of iodine is suitable for this investigation.

Answers

	Marks
6 See Table 8.	5

Table 8

Time (minutes)	Tube A	Tube B	Tube C	Tube D
0	✓ ✓	✓ ✓	✓ ✓	✓ ✓
3	✓ ✓	✓	✓ ✓	✓ ✓
6	✓ ✓	0	✓ ✓	✓ ✓
9	✓	0	✓ ✓	✓ ✓
12	✓	0	✓ ✓	✓ ✓

7 Tubes A and B. — 2

8 (a) An enzyme. — 1
   (b) Amylase. — 1
   (c) The enzyme in solution Y is inactive. — 1
   (d) The enzyme in solution Y has been denatured, either by boiling or by adding a toxic chemical compound. — 1

9 (a) Tubes A and B contain active enzyme. Differences in temperature account for differences in the rate of reaction in the two tubes. In tube A, surrounded by iced water, the rate of reaction is much slower than in tube B, where the temperature is 40 °C. — 2
   (b) Tube B contains active enzyme, but tube C contains enzyme that has been denatured. Although both tubes are maintained under the same conditions, only the active enzyme catalyses the breakdown of starch. — 2

10 (a) Tube D was set up to show that starch, mixed with water, does not undergo any chemical change. — 1
   (b) Water was added to tube D to bring the total volume of liquid to 10 cm^3, as in tubes A, B, and C. — 1

11 (a) Tubes were shaken to ensure that any starch grains in the liquids were suspended. — 1
   (b) Additional liquid from the straws might have diluted the mixtures, making results difficult to interpret. — 1
   (c) Any remaining starch grains must be removed from the rod before each test is carried out. The rod must be dried so that the mixtures are not diluted by adding water. — 1

10 The effect of different temperatures on trypsin activity

TIME
Investigation: 60–80 minutes

Skills tested: 5, 6, 7, 8, 9, 10, 11, 12, 13, 16.

Materials

- 45 cm^3 milk suspension ■ 45 cm^3 trypsin solution (2) ■ Four 250 cm^3 glass beakers ■ Two 5 cm^3 plastic syringes ■ Eight small test tubes ■ Three tripods and gauzes ■ Four thermometers ■ Bunsen burner ■ Stop-clock, or watch with a second hand ■ Glass-marking pen.

Instructions and notes

1. A milk suspension that is rapidly digested by trypsin may be prepared by adding 4 g Marvel powdered milk to 100 cm^3 water.
2. Prepare the trypsin solution by dissolving 0.5 g pancreatic extract in 100 cm^3 water.
3. Water baths, suitable for this investigation, can be made from tins that have contained milk powder.

Answers

Marks

5 See Table 9.   4

Table 9

Tube No.	Time for completion of reaction (minutes)
1	16
3	8
5	4
7	24 (some not completed)

6 (a) Room temperature $+20\,°C$.   1
   (b) Room temperature $+50\,°C$.   1
   (c) Above temperatures of 40–45 °C, enzymes are denatured, and lose their ability to act as catalysts.   2
7 (a) Investigations were limited to rates of reaction at only four different temperatures.   1
   (b) The investigation could have been extended to find rates of reaction over a broader range of temperature, e.g. 0, 10, 20, 30, 40, 50, 60, 70, 80, 90 and 100 °C.   2
8 See Table 10.   4

Table 10

Tube No.	Time for completion of reaction (minutes)
2	6
4	4
6	3
8	Not completed

9 The enzyme's activity is reduced: some of its molecules are denatured.   1
10 Dissolve some washing powder (e.g. 1 g) in 100 cm^3 water. Prepare a suspension of milk powder. Put 5 cm^3 of each solution into each of eight test tubes. Incubate one of the tubes at each of the following temperatures: 20, 25, 30, 35, 40, 45, 50, and 55 °C. Record the time taken for the mixture in each tube to become colourless. The optimum temperature is the one at which the mixture clears most rapidly.   4

11 Measuring enzyme activity by gas production

TIME
Investigation: 30–40 minutes

Skills tested: 5, 6, 7, 8, 9, 10, 11, 12, 13, 14.

Materials

■ Suspension of yeast cells, with added detergent ■ 50 cm^3 hydrogen peroxide solution ■ 50 cm^3 distilled water ■ Iron filings (on a labelled-sheet of paper) ■ Granules of dried yeast (on a labelled-sheet of paper) ■ Seven test tubes, in a rack ■ Spatula ■ Ruler, graduated in millimetres ■ Glass-marking pen ■ Safety spectacles ■ Plastic gloves ■ Graph paper

Instructions and notes

1 Prepare the yeast suspension from the following materials:
10 g dried yeast
5 cm^3 washing-up fluid
100 cm^3 water
2 If fresh stocks of hydrogen peroxide are available, a 2–vol solution is suitable for this investigation. If stocks have been in the laboratory for some time, and there has been deterioration, a 5–vol solution should be used.

> **Pupils should wear safety spectacles, plastic gloves, and laboratory coats when handling hydrogen peroxide. They should be warned that the compound can cause burns and bleaching, unless immediately washed off with plenty of water.**

3 All of the test tubes used in this investigation should be of uniform size, preferably not more than 1.25 cm in width.

Answers

Part A
Marks

1. (a) Bubbles of gas were produced.   1
   (b) The iron filings act as a catalyst, breaking down hydrogen peroxide into oxygen and water.   2
   (c) Bubbles of gas were produced, but at a faster rate than when iron filings were used.   1
   (d) The dried yeast contains catalase, an enzyme that catalyses the breakdown of hydrogen peroxide into oxygen and water.   2

Part B

2. See Table 11.   2

Table 11

Tube No.	1	2	3	4	5
Height of bubble column (cm)	0.9	1.5	2.1	2.7	3.3

3. See Figure 10.   4

Fig. 10 *Bar graph, showing the height of bubble columns in the tubes*

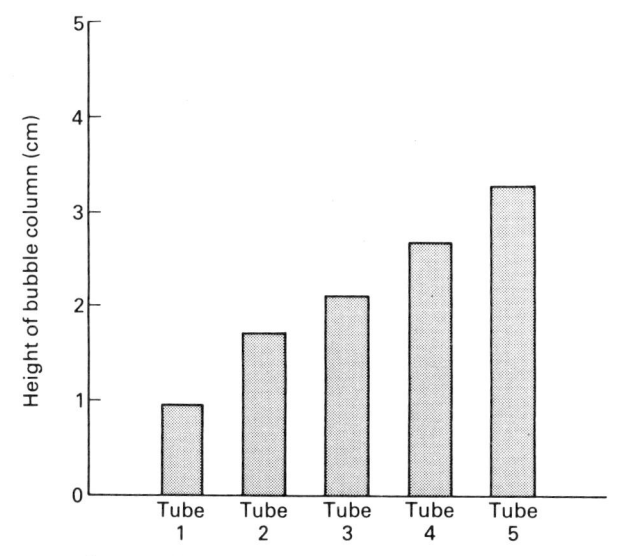

4. Yeast suspension, to show no bubbles were formed in the absence of hydrogen peroxide.   2

Part C

5 Take five test tubes and number them from 1–5. Return the tubes to a rack. Using a syringe, pipette 2.0 cm³ hydrogen peroxide solution into each tube. With a clean syringe, add different volumes of yeast suspension to the tubes, as follows:
Tube 1: 0.5 cm³   Tube 4: 2.0 cm³
Tube 2: 1.0 cm³   Tube 5: 2.5 cm³
Tube 3: 1.5 cm³
As soon as a froth has formed, measure the height of the column of bubbles above the mixture in each tube. Record your results in the form of a table, and plot a bar graph.   6

12 Using enzymes to extract fruit juice: an introduction to biotechnology

TIME
Preparation: 15–20 minutes
Investigation: 30–40 minutes

Skills tested: 5, 6, 7, 8, 13, 15, 16.

Materials

Preparation

- 400 cm³ apple purée, in a beaker
- Pectolytic enzyme powder
- Cellulase enzyme powder (6)
- Four 100 cm³ measuring cylinders
- Two 100 cm³ beakers
- Four filter funnels
- Four filter papers
- Tea spoon
- Tissue paper
- Glass-marking pen

Investigation

- Four measuring cylinders, containing filtered apple juice

Instructions and notes

1 Apple purée may be made by grinding 500 g sliced cooking apples with 200 cm³ water in a kitchen mixer.
2 Pectolytic enzyme, sold for clearing wine, is available from branches of Boots the chemists.
3 This investigation, intended for more able pupils, is set up one day in advance.

Answers

                                                                    Marks

1 See Table 12.

   Table 12

Measuring cylinder No.	1	2	3	4
Volume (cm³) juice extracted	26	34	39	60

   4

2 (a) No. 1. 1
   (b) It contains natural apple purée, without added enzymes. 1
3 (a) Increase in volume = $34 - 26 = 8$ cm^3.
       Percentage increase in volume = $\dfrac{8 \times 100}{26} = 30.77\%$ 2
   (b) Increase in volume = $39 - 26 = 13$ cm^3
       Percentage increase in volume = $\dfrac{13 \times 100}{26} = 50\%$ 2
   (c) Increase in volume = $60 - 26 = 34$ cm^3
       Percentage increase in volume = $\dfrac{34 \times 100}{26} = 130.77\%$ 2
4 Enzyme activity is affected by temperature. Keeping the measuring cylinders in a warm place increased the rate of juice extraction. 1
5 Pectinase clears the juice, by digesting opaque material. 1
6 Additional sugar comes from the breakdown of cellulose and pectin.
7 Amounts of apple juice extracted from the purée can be increased by 1
   adding either cellulase or pectinase. Mixed together, the two enzymes have a more marked effect on juice extraction. By breaking down different parts of cell walls, they increase the rate at which juice is released from cells of the apple.

   The process is of economic importance. Addition of enzymes to purée increases the amount of juice that can be extracted from crushed fruit, sweetens the product, and improves its appearance. 5

13 Enzyme inhibition by drugs

TIME
Investigation: 40–50 minutes

Skills tested: 5, 6, 7, 8, 9, 10, 11, 12, 13, 14, 15, 16.

Materials

- Plastic beaker, containing 50 cm^3 tap water ■ 40 cm^3 starch suspension ■ 5 cm^3 ethanol ■ 5 cm^3 salicylic acid (asprin) solution (2) ■ Iodine solution ■ Eight flat-bottomed tubes ■ Four 5 cm^3 plastic syringes ■ 1 cm^3 plastic syringe ■ Stop-clock, or watch with a second hand ■ Glass-marking pen ■ Graph paper

Instructions and notes

1. The salicylic acid (asprin) solution contains 1 g dissolved in 100 cm^3 water. A slight cloudiness of the solution will not affect the result.
2. Prepare the starch suspension by mixing 10 g soluble starch to a paste with a little cold water. Add this to 1 dm^3 boiling water in a beaker. Allow the starch suspension to cool to room temperature before it is distributed. As the action of the amylase is affected by temperature, it is advisable to test the experiment to find the most suitable time for adding iodine solution to the tubes. This information should be made available to pupils before they carry out the investigation.
3. Bench iodine solution may be used. Alternatively, prepare a solution of iodine by dissolving 4.0 g potassium iodide and 0.2 g iodine in 100 cm^3 water.

Answers

Marks

3 (a) Effect of ethanol. See Table 13.

Table 13

Tube No.	1	2	3	4
Colour intensity No.	5	4	3	2

24

Effect of salicylic acid. See Table 14.

Table 14

Tube No.	1	2	3	4
Colour intensity No.	5	2	1	0

(b) See Figure 11.

Fig. 11 *Inhibition of salivary amylase by ethanol and salicylic acid*

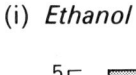

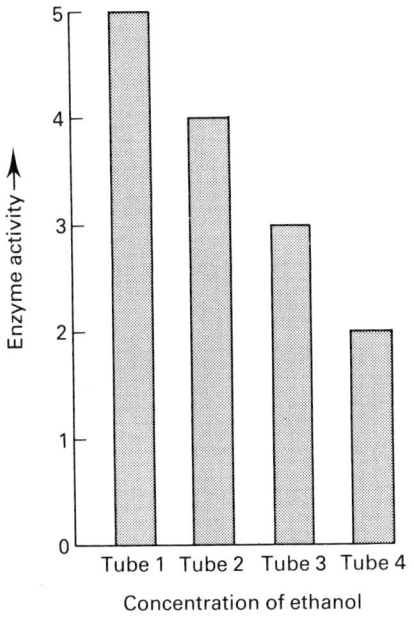

(i) *Ethanol*   (ii) *Salicylic acid*

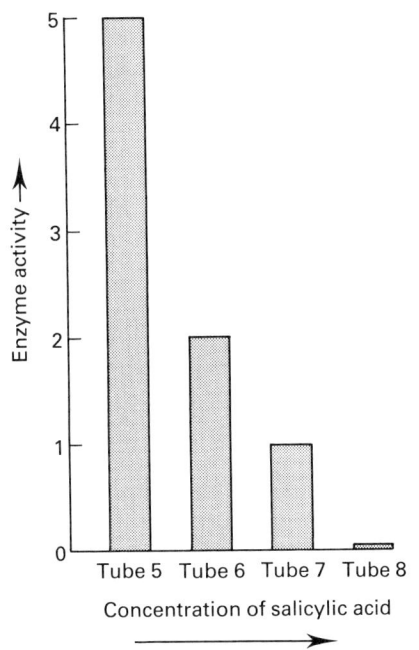

4 (a) As doses of ethanol and salicylic acid were increased, there was a corresponding decrease in amylase activity.
   (b) Salicylic acid.

5 (a) $\dfrac{0.5}{7.5} \times 100 = 6.66\,\%$

   (b) $\dfrac{2.0}{9.0} \times 100 = 22.2\,\%$

6 Each tube contained different volumes of the starch/enzyme/inhibitor mixture. The design could have been improved by adding water to tubes 1–3 and 5–7 to increase the volume in each tube to $9.0\,\text{cm}^3$.

14 Sugar, bacteria and tooth decay

TIME
Investigation: 30–40 minutes

Skills tested: 5, 6, 9, 10, 14, 18, 19, 20.

Materials

- Two cotton buds, in a clean petri dish ■ Tooth paste, on a white tile ■ Universal indicator, in a dropping bottle (2) ■ Universal indicator colour chart

Instructions and notes

1. Prepare the indicator by adding 5 cm^3 Universal Indicator to 100 cm^3 distilled water. Each pupil will require approximately 5 cm^3 in a dropping bottle.
2. Each pupil will require a small amount of toothpaste on a white tile.

> At the end of the investigation, petri dishes containing the cotton buds should be collected, put into a heat-resistant bag, and incinerated.

Answers

Part A   Marks

1. (a) Red.   1
   (b) pH 4.0–5.5.   1
   (c) Acid   1
   (d) The acid has been formed from sugars in the diet.   1
   (e) Enzymes from bacteria have changed the sugar into acid.   1
   (f) Teeth should be brushed from side-to-side and up-and-down. Bacteria collect close to the gum and between the teeth. They must be brushed in both directions if the teeth are to be properly cleaned.   2

2 (a) pH 7.5. 1
   (b) The toothpaste is slightly alkaline. This helps to neutralise any acid produced by bacteria on the surfaces of the teeth. 2

Part B

3 (a) There is a direct relationship between the number of acid-forming bacteria in a person's mouth, and the number of dental fillings they receive. 2
   (b) Count and record the number of dental fillings in each pupil. Collect 5 cm^3 saliva from each pupil and add it to 5 cm^3 sucrose solution, in a petri dish. Incubate each mixture at 37°C, and record changes in pH. Draw graphs to show the rate at which bacteria in the saliva of each pupil changes sucrose to acid. 4
   (c) If the hypothesis is correct, pupils with the most fillings will form acid from sucrose more rapidly than those with fewer fillings. 2
   (d) See Figure 12. 2

Fig. 12 *Relationship between the number of fillings and the rate of acid formation*

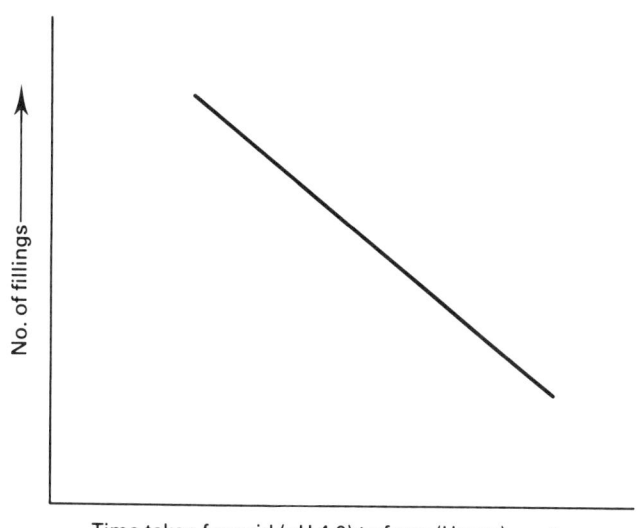

[Graph: y-axis "No. of fillings", x-axis "Time taken for acid (pH 4.0) to form (Hours)", showing a straight line with negative slope.]

15 Demonstrating and making use of diffusion

TIME
Preparation: 15–20 minutes
Investigation: 30–40 minutes

Skills tested: 5, 6, 7, 8, 9, 10, 13, 15, 16

Materials

Preparation

■ Three Universal Indicator agar plates (2) ■ DCPIP agar plate (2) ■ 5 cm^3 vitamin C (ascorbic acid) solution (2) ■ 5 cm^3 distilled water ■ Dilute bench hydrochloric acid, in a dropping bottle ■ Dilute bench sodium hydroxide solution, in a dropping bottle ■ Concentrated ammonia solution, and glass rod ■ Three flat-bottomed tubes, approximately 2 × 8 cm ■ Three 1 cm^3 plastic syringes ■ Cork borer (No. 5, 6, or 7) ■ Glass-marking pen ■ Safety spectacles

Investigation

■ Three Universal Indicator agar plates ■ DCPIP agar plate, containing vitamin C solutions

Instructions and notes

1. The vitamin C solution contains 4 g ascorbic acid dissolved in 100 cm^3 water.
2. When preparing the agar plates, it is important to use bacteriological agar powder, or another purified agar.
   Universal Indicator agar: 100 cm^3 distilled water, 2.5 g powder.
   Mix the agar powder with a little cold water to form a slurry, and add this to boiling water. Cool to 60–80°C before adding 5 cm^3 Universal Indicator, stirring to ensure even distribution. Pour the molten agar into petri dishes, to a depth of 3–4 mm.
   DCPIP agar: 100 cm^3 distilled water, 2.5 g agar powder, 0.01 g DCPIP.
   Mix the dye and agar powder with a little cold water to form a slurry, and add this to boiling water, stirring to ensure even distribution. Pour the molten agar into petri dishes to a depth of 3–4 nm.
3. The solutions should be applied to the agar plates approximately 30 minutes before the assessment.

Answers

Part A
                                                                    Marks

1 (a) Blue.   1
   (b) Ammonia is alkaline, and Universal Indicator is a pH indicator.   1
   (c) Molecules of ammonia have diffused through the air to reach the plate.   1
   (d) The drop of ammonia is surrounded by a purple/blue circle.   1
   (e) Ammonia has diffused from the drop into the agar.   1
2 (a) Red, fringed by yellow/orange.   2
   (b) Purple, fringed by blue.   2
   (c) The larger circle formed around the well containing hydrochloric acid.   1
   (d) Ions/molecules in hydrochloric acid diffuse faster than those in sodium hydroxide solution.
Ions/molecules in hydrochloric acid are more concentrated than those in sodium hydroxide solution.   1

Part B
3 See Table 15.   4

Table 15

Well No.	1	2	3	4
Concentration of vitamin C (g/100 cm^3)	4.0	2.0	1.0	0.5
Radius of circle (cm)	0.9	0.6	0.5	0.4
Area of circle (cm^2)	2.54	1.13	0.78	0.5

4 Cut a fifth well in the DCPIP agar and place two drops of lemon juice into it. Allow diffusion to occur for 30–40 minutes, then measure the radius from the centre of the well to the edge of the circle cleared of dye. Use the formula πr^2 to calculate the total area cleared of dye. Plot a graph of the areas cleared of dye (vertical axis) against concentrations of vitamin C in wells 1–4 (horizontal axis). Draw a vertical line from the area of the circle surrounding lemon juice to the horizontal axis. The point at which this line crosses the horizontal axis gives the approximate vitamin C content of the lemon juice.   5

16 Diffusion of water through natural and artificial membranes

TIME
Preparation: 20–30 minutes
Investigation: 30–40 minutes

Skills tested: 5, 6, 7, 8, 13, 15, 16.

Materials

Preparation

- 25 g currants ■ 25 g sultanas ■ 25 g prunes ■ 15 cm length of dialysis tubing (4, 5) ■ 10 cm^3 starch/glucose mixture ■ 20 cm^3 distilled water ■ Boiling tube ■ 250 cm^3 beaker ■ Three 100 cm^3 beakers ■ String ■ Paper tissues ■ Top-pan balance ■ Glass-marking pen

Investigation

- Apparatus containing dialysis tubing and starch/glucose mixture ■ Currants, sultanas and prunes, soaked in water ■ Iodine solution (for starch testing) ■ Clinistix reagent strip ■ White tile ■ Glass rod ■ Paper tissues ■ Top-pan balance

Instructions and notes

1. The starch/glucose mixture contains 2 g soluble starch and 5 g glucose, mixed to a slurry with a little cold water. This is added to 100 cm^3 boiling water. Allow the mixture to cool before it is distributed.
2. Bench iodine solution may be used in this investigation.
3. Pupils may either be supplied with 25 g lots of each dried fruit, or they may weigh their own samples during the preparation.
4. Dialysis tubing should be of a smaller diameter than the boiling tube. It is advisable to soak the dialysis tubing in warm water for 1–5 minutes before it is distributed. If this is not done, pupils may have difficulties in opening the tubing.
5. Dialysis tubing should be set up, and dried fruits soaked in water, approximately 24 hours before the investigation.

Answers

Part A
Marks

1 Washing would remove any starch or glucose spilled over the outside of the dialysis tubing during filling. — 1
2 (a) Glucose present. — 1
 (b) Starch absent. — 1
 (c) Glucose molecules are much smaller than those of starch. The tubing is permeable to glucose, but not to starch. Hence, only glucose molecules can diffuse to the outside. — 2
3 (a) Original mass of dialysis tubing and starch/glucose mixture = 11.0 g
 Mass after standing for 24 hours = 13.5 g — 1
 (b) Percentage increase in mass = $\dfrac{2.5}{11.0} \times 100 = 22.7\%$ — 2
 (c) Water has diffused from the boiling tube into the dialysis tubing. This additional water has increased the mass of the dialysis tubing and its contents. — 2
 (d) More water would have entered the tubing. — 1

Part B

4 See Table 16. — 2

Table 16

Fruit	Currants	Sultanas	Prunes
Mass (g)	37.5	33.6	45.3

5 Percentage increase in mass of currants = $\dfrac{12.5}{25} \times 100 = 50\%$ — 1

Percentage increase in mass of sultanas = $\dfrac{8.6 \times 100}{25} = 34.4\%$ — 1

Percentage increase in mass of prunes = $\dfrac{20.3 \times 100}{25} = 81.2\%$ — 1

6 Currants. — 1
7 Prunes. More water diffused into the prunes than into the currants or sultanas. — 2
8 There is insufficient water in dried fruit to support bacteria or fungi. High concentrations of sugar cause water to diffuse from the bodies of micro-organisms, causing desiccation and leading to death. — 1

17 Water loss from leaves

TIME
Investigation: 60–90 minutes

Skills tested: 5, 6, 7, 8, 13, 15, 16, 17.

Materials

- Five leaves of cherry laurel ■ Cobalt chloride paper ■ Vaseline
- Cotton wool ■ Adhesive tape ■ Forceps ■ Scissors ■ Clock, or watch ■ Top-pan balance ■ Glass-marking pen

Instructions and notes

1. Freshly-picked leaves of cherry laurel, or some other large-leaved species, are required for this investigation. Four of the leaves given to each pupil should be of approximately the same size.
2. Cobalt chloride paper may be prepared by painting a solution of the salt on to filter paper. The paper is dried in front of a fan heater, or over a radiator. It may be kept in a dessicator until it is distributed. Each pupil will require three pieces, approximately 1 cm^2, supplied in a closed container, such as a petri dish.
3. Translucent adhesive tape, 2.5 cm or more in width, should be used to cover pieces of cobalt chloride paper.
4. The top-pan balance should weigh in units of 0.01 g.

Answers

Marks

Part A

1 See Table 17. 5

2 (a) $3.00 - 2.80 = 0.20$.
   (b) $2.91 - 2.73 = 0.18$.
   (c) $3.31 - 3.28 = 0.03$.
   (d) $3.30 - 3.29 = 0.01$. 2

Table 17

Time (minutes)	Mass of leaves (g)			
	Leaf 1	Leaf 2	Leaf 3	Leaf 4
0	3.00	2.91	3.31	3.30
15	2.92	2.83	3.30	3.30
30	2.86	2.78	3.29	3.30
45	2.80	2.73	3.28	3.29

3 $\dfrac{0.20}{3.00} \times 100 = 6.66\%$ 2

4 More water was lost from the lower surface of the leaf than from the upper surface. There was a loss of 0.18 g from leaf 2, compared with a loss of only 0.03 g from leaf 3. 2

5 (a) Vaseline is a water-proofing material. It blocked stomata and prevented loss of water by evaporation from epidermal cells. 1
  (b) Water can evaporate from the cut end of the leaf stalk (petiole). 1

Part B

6 See Table 18. 2

Table 18

Position of paper	Time for colour change (minutes)
Upper surface	28
Lower epidermis	5
Bench	7

Air contains water vapour. The lower epidermis is moister than the surrounding air. The lower epidermis releases more water vapour than the upper. 3

7 Weighing produced the best results, as the method was quantitative, indicating the mass of water lost from each leaf in unit periods of time. 2

18 Osmosis in living tissue

TIME
Preparation: 20–30 minutes
Investigation: 30–40 minutes

Skills tested: 5, 6, 7, 8, 11, 12, 13, 14, 15, 16.

Materials

Preparation

- Three or four large potato tubers ■ 100 cm³ of each of the following: ■ Distilled water (0.0 M), ■ 0.2 M glucose solution, ■ 0.4 M glucose solution, ■ 0.6 M glucose solution, ■ 0.8 M glucose solution, ■ 1.0 M glucose solution ■ 100 cm³ measuring cylinder ■ No. 13 cork borer ■ Six paper cups, or similar containers ■ Ruler, graduated in millimetres ■ Scalpel ■ Glass-marking pen

Investigation

- Cups, containing rods of potato tissue ■ 100 cm³ measuring cylinder ■ Ruler, graduated in millimetres ■ Graph paper

Instructions and notes

1 A molar solution of glucose contains 180 g/dm³.
2 Cups, containing rods of potato immersed in water or glucose solution, should be set up approximately 24 hours before the investigation.

Answers

                                                                            Marks

1 See Table 19.   4

Table 19

Molarity of glucose solution	0.0	0.2	0.4	0.6	0.8	1.0
Volume of liquid in cup (cm³)	84	88	93	95	95	95

2 See Figure 13. 4

Fig. 13 *Effect of the concentration of glucose on water movement in rods of potato tissue*

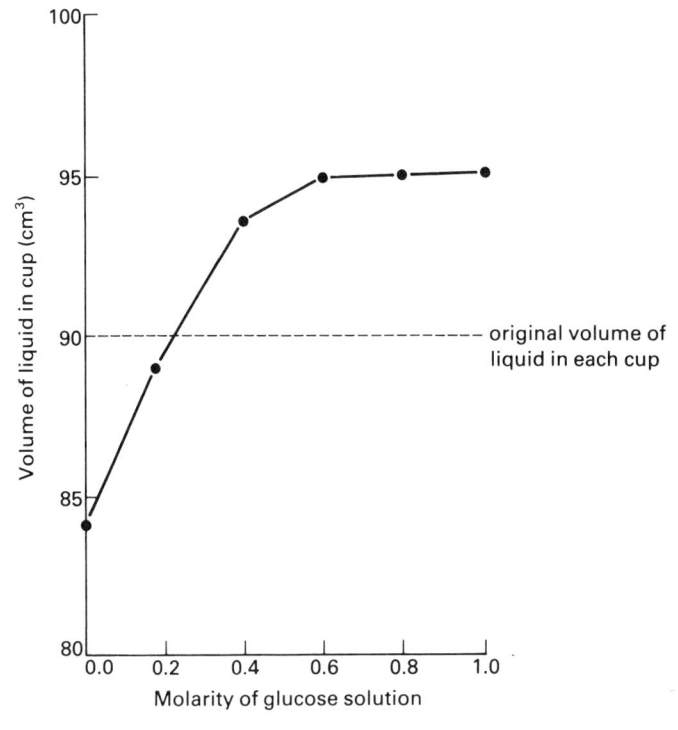

[Graph: Volume of liquid in cup (cm³) on y-axis (80–100) vs. Molarity of glucose solution on x-axis (0.0–1.0). Curve rises from ~84 at 0.0, through ~89 at 0.2, ~94 at 0.4, to ~95 at 0.6, 0.8, and 1.0. Dashed horizontal line at 90 labelled "original volume of liquid in each cup".]

3 See Table 20. 4

Table 20

Molarity of glucose solution	0.0	0.2	0.4	0.6	0.8	1.0
Length of rod (cm)	3.3	3.1	2.9	2.7	2.7	2.7

4 (a) Cup 1. 1
  (b) Cups 3, 4, 5, and 6. 2
  (c) Cup 2. 1

5 Water flows in both directions. The inward flow of water is equal to the outward flow. Therefore, there is no net movement of water. 2

6 Cover the cups to prevent loss of water by evaporation. Use a clean, dry measuring cylinder when measuring the volume of liquid in each cup. By using the same measuring cylinder, some liquid will remain from previous measurements. Weigh the rods, after drying them on a paper tissue, to obtain a more accurate indication of water movement. 2

19 Using a simple potometer

TIME
Investigation: 30–40 minutes

Skills tested: 5, 6, 7, 8, 13, 14, 15, 16.

Materials

- Cut shoot of a large-leaved woody plant, bearing two leaves ■ 100 cm^3 beaker, containing tap water ■ Simple potometer (5) ■ Retort stand, boss, and clamp ■ Rubber tubing ■ Ruler, graduated in millimeters ■ Bench lamp, fitted with a 60 W bulb ■ Stop-clock, or watch with a second hand ■ Glass-marking pen ■ Graph paper

Instructions and notes

1 The cut ends of the shoots should be immersed in water immediately after cutting.
2 When the cut shoots are distributing to pupils, their cut ends should be immersed in the beaker of water.
3 All leaves, with the exception of the two largest, should be removed from the shoots before they are distributed.
4 Capillary tubing forming part of the potometer should be 0.2 cm in diameter.
5 Rubber tubing, cut into 1–2 cm lengths, should be of a diameter suitable for fixing the cut end of a shoot into the side arm of the potometer.
6 The nature, and method of applying an aerosol antitranspirant, may be demonstrated before the investigation.

Answers

Marks

1 See Table 21. 3

Table 21

No. leaves on shoot	2	1	0
Distance travelled by meniscus (cm)	0.9	0.5	0.2

2 See Figure 14. 5

Fig. 14 *Relationship between water uptake and the number of leaves removed from a cut shoot*

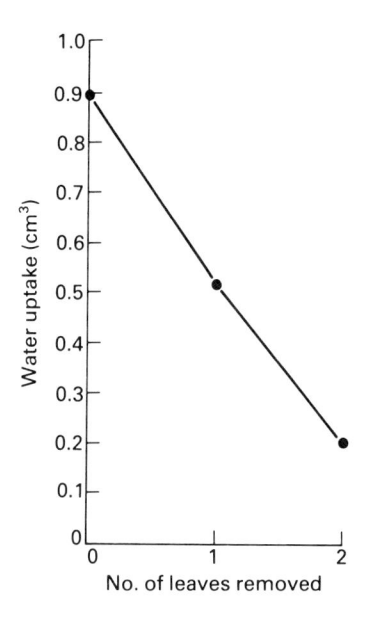

3 (a) Light from the lamp caused stomata to open. 1
   (b) Heat from the lamp caused water to evaporate more rapidly. 1
4 $3.14 \times 0.1 \times 0.1 \times 0.9 = 0.002826$ cm^3 2
5 (a) Yes. 1
   (b) Some water is lost via lenticels in the bark. Additional water is lost via the cut ends of xylem vessels. 2
6 (a) Leaves, or 'needles' of Christmas trees fall because they dry out and die in a hot atmosphere. By reducing water loss, the antitranspirant keeps more leaves alive, reducing the rate of leaf fall. 2
   (b) Unrooted cuttings may lose water faster than they take it up. By restricting water loss the antitranspirant keeps the cutting alive until it has a chance to develop a root system. 2
7 Prolonging the vase-life of cut flowers. Preventing wilting in greenhouse crops. 1

20 Factors affecting the rate of photosynthesis

TIME
Investigation: 40–50 minutes
April–October

Skills tested: 5, 6, 7, 8, 13, 14, 16.

Materials

- Two cut shoots of Canadian pondweed
- 5 cm³ sodium hydrogen carbonate (bicarbonate) solution
- 1 dm³ beaker
- 1 cm³ plastic syringe
- Two glass rods
- Cotton
- Thermometer
- Tripod and gauze
- Bunsen burner
- Scissors
- Stop-clock, or watch with a second hand
- Graph paper

Instructions and notes

1 The sodium hydrogen carbonate (bicarbonate) solution contains 2 g dissolved in 100 cm³ distilled water.
2 Shoots of Canadian pondweed should be freshly cut from plants that are actively photosynthesising.

Answers

	Marks
3 See Table 22.	2
4 See Figure 15.	4
5 See Table 23.	2
6 See Figure 16.	4
7 See Table 24	2
8 See Figure 17.	4

Table 22

Distance of light source from plant (cm)	5	10	20	30
No. bubbles/min	28	24	18	10

Fig. 15 *Relationship between the rate of photosynthesis and the position of a light source*

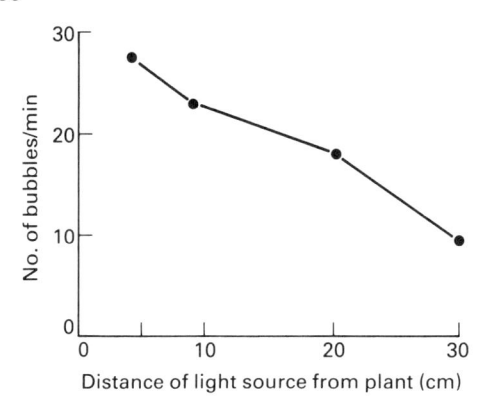

Table 23

Vol. sodium hydrogen carbonate solution added (cm^3)	0	0.25	0.75	1.75	3.75
No. bubbles/min	28	36	44	60	64

Fig. 16 *Relationship between the rate of photosynthesis and sodium hydrogen carbonate concentration*

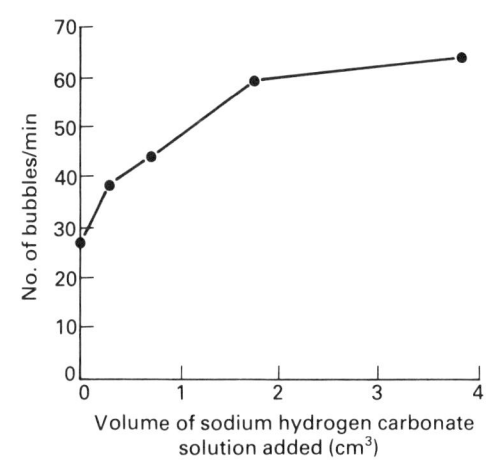

Table 24

Temperature (°C)	20	30	40	50	60
No. bubbles/min	85	128	196	73	0

Fig. 17 *Relationship between rate of photosynthesis and temperature*

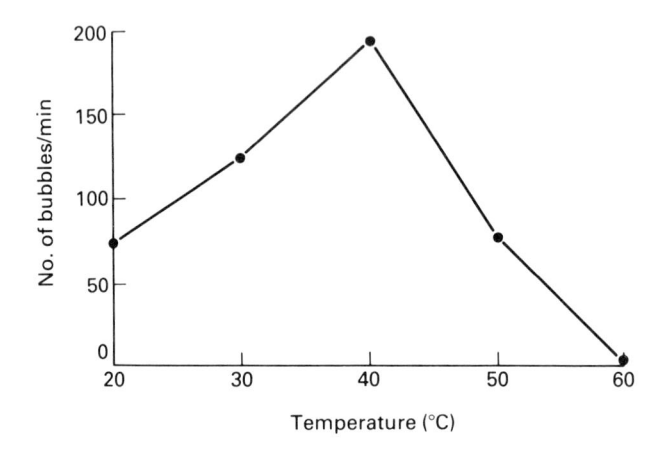

9 The reactions that occur during photosynthesis are controlled by enzymes. Between 20 °C and 40 °C, the rate of photosynthesis is increased, until the optimal temperature for enzyme activity is reached. Above 40 °C, however, enzymes were denatured, so that they could no longer catalyse those reactions that resulted in the production of gas.   2

21 Gas production by Canadian pondweed during photosynthesis

TIME
Investigation: 40–50 minutes
April–October

Skills tested: 5, 6, 7, 8, 9, 10, 13, 14.

Materials

- Living leafy shoots of Canadian pondweed
- 25 cm^3 sodium hydrogen carbonate (bicarbonate) solution
- 20 cm^3 plastic syringe
- 100 cm^3 beaker
- 30 cm length of 0.1 mm diameter capillary tubing
- Rubber tubing (to fit over capillary and nozzle of syringe)
- Boss, clamp, and retort stand
- Bench lamp, fitted with 100 W bulb
- Scalpel
- Ruler, graduated in millimetres
- Glass-marking pen

Instructions and notes

1 Preparation of the sodium hydrogen carbonate (bicarbonate) solution is described in Investigation 20.
2 If satisfactory results are to be obtained, it is essential to have an abundant supply of living Canadian pondweed, freshly harvested from a pond.

Answers

                                                           Marks

1 See Table 25.   4

Table 25

Distance of lamp from syringe (cm)	5	10	15	20
Distance travelled by meniscus (cm)	3.1	1.6	0.6	0.2

2 (a) See Figure 18. 4

Fig. 18 *Relationship between light intensity and the rate of photosynthesis*

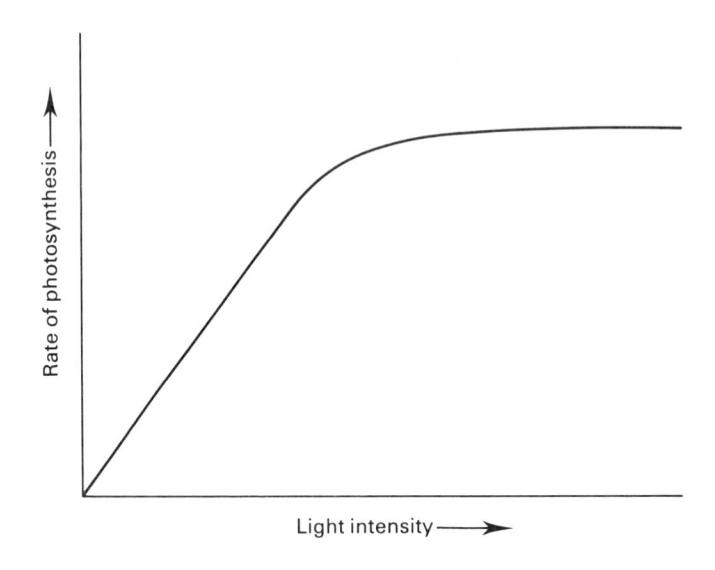

[Graph showing rate of photosynthesis (Y axis) against light intensity (X axis): curve rises linearly then levels off to a plateau.]

(b) A plot of distance travelled by the meniscus (Y axis) against distance from the light source (X axis) produces a mirror image of the curve shown in Figure 18. 2

3 (a) The amount of gas produced by three cut shoots is greater than that produced by one. By using three shoots it was possible to take readings at fairly short intervals of time. 2
  (b) Sodium hydrogen carbonate (bicarbonate) solution is a source of carbon dioxide, one of the raw materials required for photosynthesis. 2
  (c) A 100 W electric light bulb produces light of high intensity. The rate of photosynthesis in plants illuminated by this bulb is faster than in these illuminated by 40 W or 60 W bulbs. 2

4 Fit the 20 W bulb to the lamp, and place it at a fixed distance from a syringe containing shoots of Canadian pondweed. Record the distance travelled by the meniscus in 5 minutes. Fix, in turn, the 40 W, 60 W, and 100 W bulbs. Place the lamp at the same fixed distance from the plants. Record the distance travelled by the meniscus in 5 minutes, when each bulb is illuminated. Plot a graph of the wattage of the bulbs (X axis) against the distance travelled by the meniscus (Y axis). 4

22 Visits by bees to flowers

TIME
Preparation: 15–20 minutes
Observation: 2 days
Investigation: 30–40 minutes
April–September

Skills tested: 4, 5, 6, 7, 13, 14, 16, 18, 23.

Materials

Preparation

- Graph paper   ■ Cardboard   ■ Glue

Observation

- Eight record sheets   ■ Stop-watch, or watch

Investigation

- Eight completed record sheets   ■ Graph paper

Instructions and notes

1. This is an investigation that pupils can prepare in their own time, possibly during week-ends, or over the period of the summer holidays.
2. Some help may need to be given in the selection of suitable sites for the field study. It is important that sites should be accessible at all times.
3. For information on honeybees see Butler or Frisch in Further reading.

> **Permission may have to be sought from landowners. Destructive sampling of flowers from parks and municipal gardens is to be avoided at all costs.**

Answers

                     Marks

1 (a) See Figure 19.   4

Fig. 19 *Relationship between the time of day and the number of bees visiting a flower patch on a sunny, calm day*

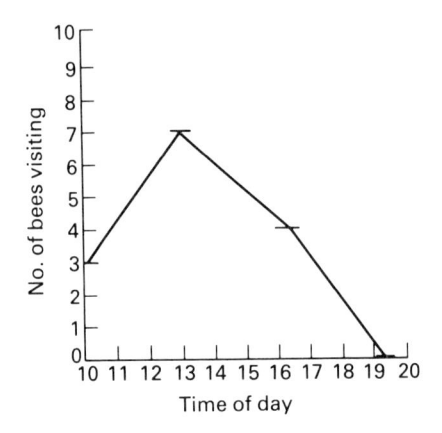

 (b) See Figure 20.   4

Fig. 20 *Relationship between the time of day and the number of bees visiting a flower patch on a dull, calm day*

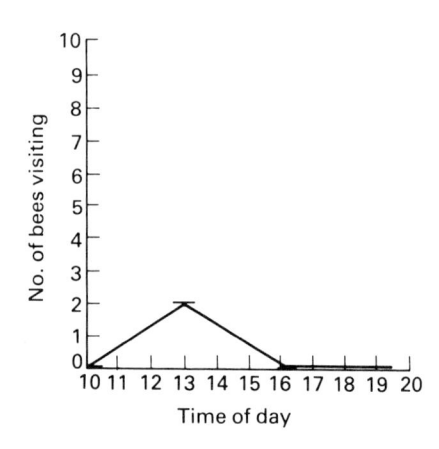

2 (a) Hive bees. 1
  (b) Most bees visited the flowers during the sunny, calm day. 1
  (c) Bees navigate by the sun, and can only find their way to and from the hive when there are some breaks in the cloud cover. Bees are cold-blooded (poikilothermic) animals. Their level of activity is influenced by temperature of the air, so that they are more likely to be active during a sunny day than a dull one. 2
  (d) Most bees visited the flowers from 13.00–13.15. 1
  (e) This was the warmest, sunniest part of the day. 1
3 Wind would reduce the total number of visits by bees. Bees, with a small body mass, would find difficulties in flying during strong winds. They may be blown off-course, or be unable to land on flowers. 2
4 Award marks for the neatness and accuracy of the record sheets. 4

23 Floral structure of tulip and polyanthus flowers

TIME
Investigation: 30–40 minutes
March–May

Skills tested: 1, 3, 5, 6

Materials

- Two flowers of tulip, labelled A
- Two flowers of polyanthus, labelled B
- Scalpel
- Seeker
- Hand lens

Instructions and notes

1 Flowers of tulip should be mature, with an ovary containing developing seeds.
2 The flowers should be supplied in separate containers, such as small jam jars, with their cut ends standing in water.

Answers

Marks

1 (a) Bees, or other large insects. 1
  (b) Large, solitary flowers, with colorful petals/perianth segments. Stamens and stigmas surrounded by petals/perianth segments. 2

2 See Table 26. 10
3 See Figure 21. 5
   See Figure 22. 2

Table 26

Feature	Flower A	Flower B
(a)	Free	Joined
(b)	5	
(c)	Receptacle	Petals
(d)	Superior	Superior
(e)	Monocotyledon	Dicotyledon

Fig. 21 *Half-flower of tulip*

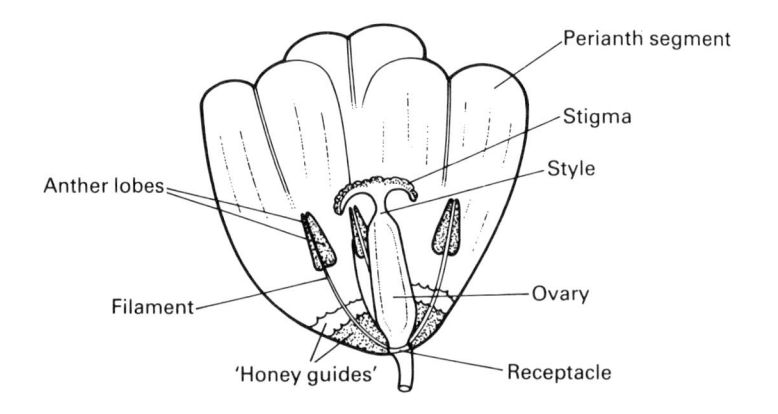

Fig. 22 *T. S. ovary of tulip*

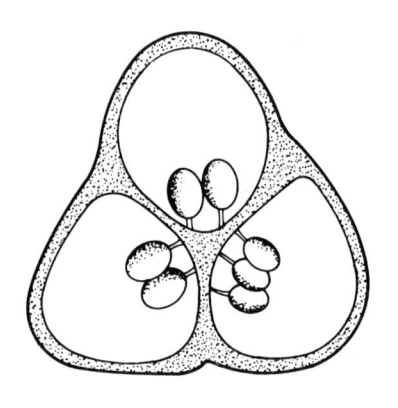

24 Wind as an agent of pollination and seed dispersal

TIME
Investigation: 30–40 minutes
July–September

Skills tested: 1, 2, 3, 5, 6.

Materials

- Inflorescence of grass, labelled A
- Inflorescence of plantain, labelled B
- Fruit of sycamore or maple, labelled C
- Fruit of poppy, labelled D
- Hand lens
- Mounted needle

Instructions and notes

1 The inflorescence of grass should bear five or more mature flowers. Inflorescences of *Plantago media*, *P. lanceolata* or *P. major* are suitable for this investigation. They should be collected in June–July and supplied to pupils with their cut flower stalks immersed in water.
2 Fruits of sycamore of maple should be intact, bearing two seeds, not split into single-seeded portions. Immature fruits, collected in July, may be given.
3 The capsule of poppy, complete with flower stalk, may be a fresh specimen, or one collected during the previous autumn.

Answers

	Marks
1 See Figure 23	3
2 (a) Flowers are small and closely packed together. Petals are absent, or green/brown in colour. Stamens protrude out of the flower, and produce large amounts of light, powdery pollen. Stigmas protrude out of the flower and are feathery/plumed.	3
(b) The flower stalks are long and flexible, swaying too and fro in the wind.	2
(c) Carpels.	1

Fig. 23 *Flower of grass*

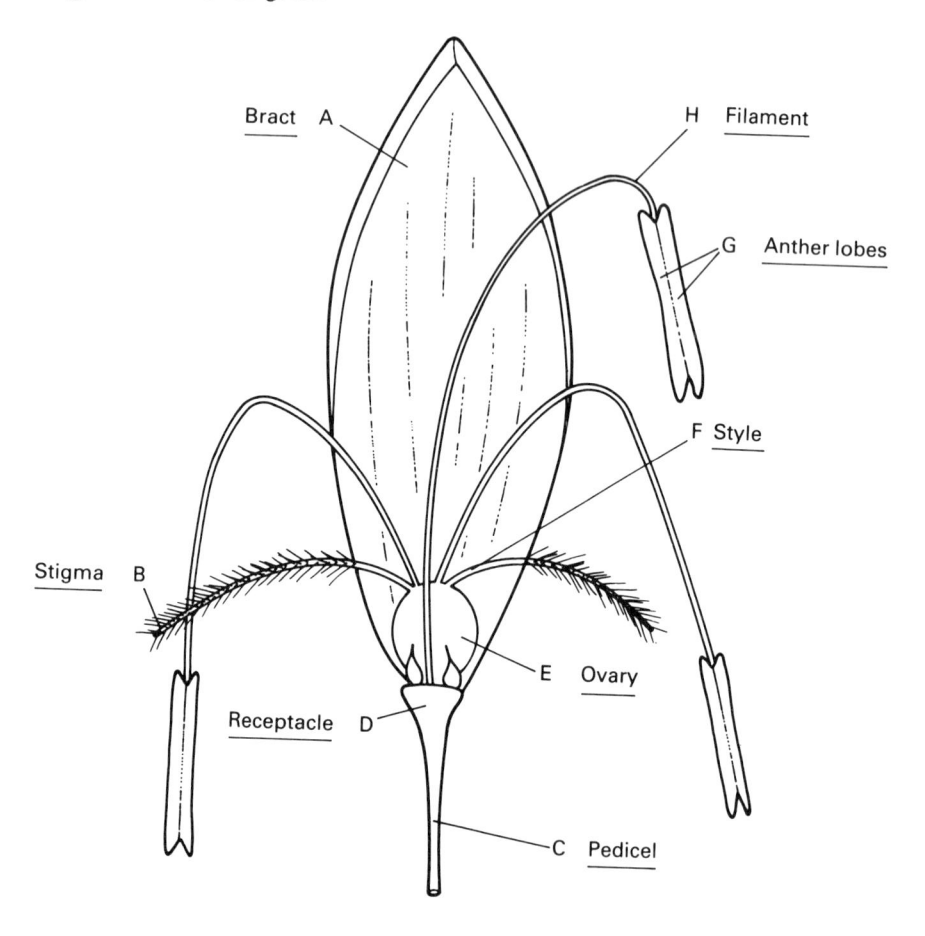

- Bract A
- H Filament
- G Anther lobes
- F Style
- Stigma B
- E Ovary
- Receptacle D
- C Pedicel

    (d) If the stamens and carpels of a flower mature at different times, self-pollination cannot occur. This is a condition that encourages self-pollination.   1

3 (a) See Figure 24.   4
    (b) The half-fruit rotated as it fell.   1
    (c) Rotation of the fruit slows its descent, enabling wind to blow the seed further from the parent plant, where it has a better chance of survival.   2

4 (a) The capsule is carried at the end of a long, flexible stalk. In strong winds the capsule bends over and the seeds are scattered from pores around the top of the capsule.   2
    (b) Partitions in the capsule prevent all the seeds from being dispersed together, or thrown in the same direction.   1

Fig. 24 *Fruit of sycamore*

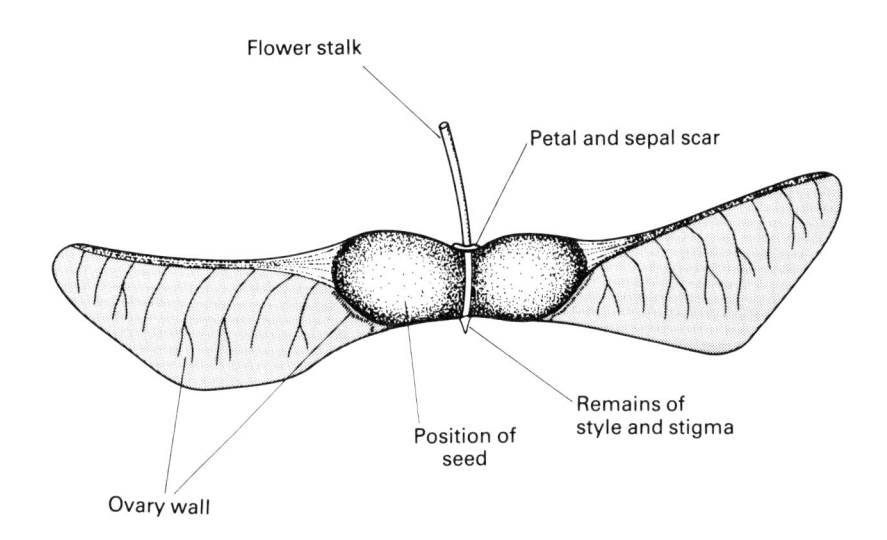

- Flower stalk
- Petal and sepal scar
- Remains of style and stigma
- Position of seed
- Ovary wall

25 Distribution of seeds around a tree

TIME
Preparation: 30–60 minutes
Investigation: 30–40 minutes
September–October

Skills tested: 6, 7, 13, 14, 15, 16, 23.

Materials

Preparation

- Four transect lines, marked at distance of 5 m
- 1 m^2 quadrat
- Eight pegs
- Magnetic compass

Investigation

- Table of results
- Graph paper

Instructions and notes

1 The transect lines can be made from 25 m lengths of coarse string, with knots tied at distances of 5 m along their length.
2 If possible, the investigation should be carried out on a large, solitary tree, growing in open ground.

Answers

	Marks
1 Data for fruits (and seeds) of lime. See Table 27.	4
2 (a) 8.	1
(b) 34.	1
(c) 93.	1
(d) 11.	1
3 (a) East.	1
(b) West.	1

Table 27

Direction	Distance from tree (m)					
	0	5	10	15	20	25
North (N)	2	2	1	2	1	0
South (S)	4	8	10	6	3	3
East (E)	8	13	20	25	18	9
West (W)	4	4	2	0	1	0

4 Winds are chiefly from a westerly direction. Therefore, most seeds are blown towards the east-facing side of the tree, with relatively few falling on the windward side.   1
5 See Figure 25.   5
6 There are few seeds around the trunk, because leaves and branches prevent them from falling in this area. Most seeds are found immediately outside the border of the leaf canopy, where leaves do not impede their fall. Numbers of seeds decrease with increasing distance from the edge of the canopy, as wind must carry them into this position.   2
7 The greatest distance over which a seed is dispersed.
The period of time over which dispersal occurs.   2

Fig. 25 *Distribution of seeds on the east-facing side of a tree*

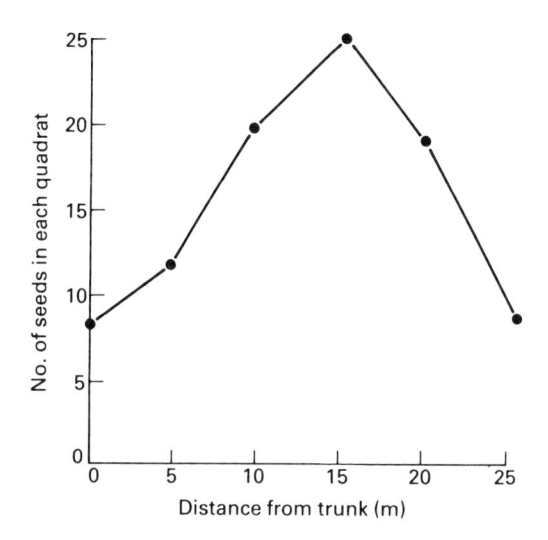

26 Depth of sowing and its effects on germination

TIME
Preparation: 15–20 minutes
Observation: 3–6 weeks
Investigation: 30–40 minutes
April–September

Skills tested: 5, 6, 7, 8, 13, 14, 16, 18.

Materials

Preparation

- Forty seeds of French bean
- Four flower pots, 15 cm in depth
- John Innes compost
- Ruler, graduated in millimetres
- Glass-marking pen

Investigation

- Record of results
- Graph paper

Instructions and notes

1. The flower pots should be 15 cm deep; the width of the pot is not important.
2. If John Innes seed or potting composts are not available, good garden top-soil may be used.
3. This investigation should be prepared 4–6 weeks before the assessment. It may be used as an individual project, to be completed during the summer holidays. If greenhouse space is not available, the pots may be put into a large polythene bag, tied with string, and left in a suitable position out of doors.

Answers

	Marks
1 (a) See Table 28.	2

Table 28

Depth of sowing (cm)	0	5	10	15
Percentage of germination	60	100	90	50

(b) See Table 29.   2

Table 29

Depth of sowing (cm)	0	5	10	15
Time taken for 5 seedlings to emerge (days)	5	7	10	12

2 See Figures 26 and 27.   6

3 (a) 5 cm.   1
  (b) 5 cm.   1
  (c) There was 100% germination of seeds sown at 5 cm, and the time taken for emergence was 7 days. Seeds sown deeper took longer to emerge.   2

4 Seeds sown at the surface were more likely to dry out than those sown more deeply. Animals that feed on seeds are more likely to find exposed seeds than those that are buried.   2

5 Deeply-planted seeds may use up their food supply before making enough growth to break through the surface of the soil. They may fail to germinate through lack of oxygen.   2

6 Slugs or snails; fungi.   2

Fig. 26 *Effect of the depth of sowing on the percentage of germination*

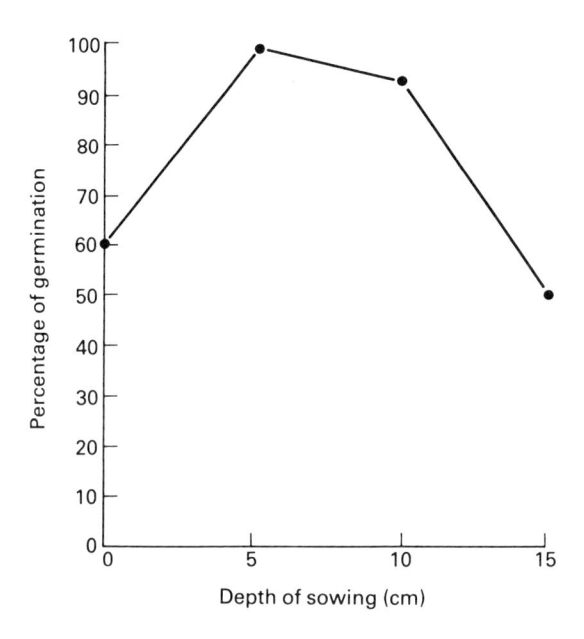

Fig. 27 *Effect of the depth of sowing on the time taken for seedlings to emerge*

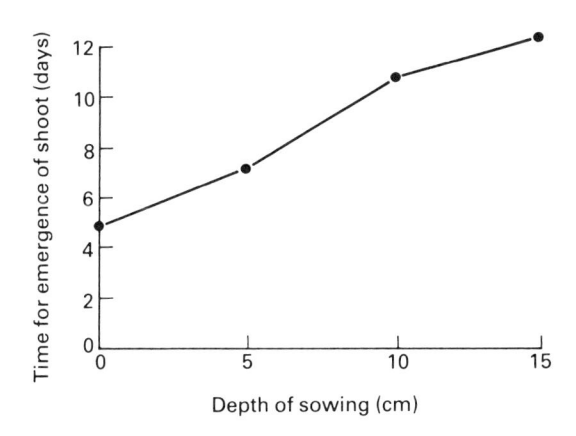

27 Producing new plants from stem cuttings

TIME
Preparation: 10–15 minutes
Observation: 2–4 weeks
Investigation: 30–40 minutes

Skills tested: 5, 6, 7, 13, 16.

Materials

Preparation

- Twelve cut shoots of mint, each bearing 10 or more leaves ■ Rooting hormone (containing auxin) ■ Four 250 cm^3 beakers ■ Scouring pad, or coarse glass paper ■ Glass-marking pen

Investigation

- Beakers 1, 2, 3, and 4, each with three cuttings of mint. ■ Record of results

Instructions and notes

1. If mint is not available, similar results can be obtained with cuttings of busy lizzie (*Impatiens*)
2. Rooting powders and liquids are available from garden centres. The label will indicate if the preparation contains auxin (IAA), or another hormone. Carry out preliminary trials to find a concentration that promotes rooting. *If too much auxin is added to the water, rooting will be inhibited.*
3. Each pupil will require approximately 100 cm^2 bench space in a greenhouse. If this is not available, each beaker may be put inside a polythene bag. After tying the bags with string, they may be put in a suitable place out of doors.

Answers

Marks

1 See Table 30.   5

Table 30

Time (day)	Number of roots formed			
	Beaker 1	Beaker 2	Beaker 3	Beaker 4
0				
1				
2				
3				
4				
5				
6				
7				
8				
9				
10				
11				
12				
13				
14				1
16				1
17				2
18		1		4
19		2		4
20		2	1	5
21		4	1	6
22		4	1	8
23	1	5	3	9
24	2	7	3	9
25	2	9	7	12
26	4	9	9	14
27	4	12	12	17
28	4	13	12	19
29	6	15	14	20
30	6	18	16	23

2 (a) Beakers 1 and 2.   1
  (b) Beakers 3 and 4.   1
  (c) Beakers 2 and 4.   1
3 (a) Adventitious roots appear from the nodes, then from the internode at the base of the stem.   1
  (b) Removal of leaves stimulated the growth of axillary buds.   1
4 (a) More adventitious roots formed following addition of auxin to the water. Roots developed along the internodes, and were more evenly distributed around the circumference of the stem.   3
  (b) When the stem was scratched, adventitious roots appeared more rapidly at the stem surface. Adventitious roots must break through the epidermis before they can emerge at the surface of the stem. Therefore, removal of the epidermis may speed up development of roots by removing a physical barrier.   3

5 (a) Removal of leaves from the stem reduced the rate of transpiration. Leaves were removed to ensure that the rate of water loss did not exceed the rate of water uptake. 1
 (b) The stem was pushed through coarse, gritty soil in order to scratch the epidermis. This was done to reduce the time taken for adventitious roots to emerge. 1
 (c) A polythene bag was placed over the pot to ensure that the cutting was surrounded by a moist, warm atmosphere, favourable to root development. 1
 (d) The polythene bag was filled with expired air as this is enriched with carbon dioxide. The intention was to stimulate the rate of photosynthesis, and thereby to increase the rate of growth in the cutting. 1

28 Comparing rates of growth in parts of a seedling

TIME
Preparation: 5–10 minutes
Observation: 7–10 days
Investigation: 30–40 minutes

Skills tested: 5, 6, 7, 8, 13, 16.

Materials

Preparation

- Petri dish, containing four grains of maize in agar
- Small flower pot, or adhesive tape.

Observation

- Scalafix tape (5)
- Marking ink and pen
- Ruler, graduated in millimetres

Investigation

- Record of results

Instructions and notes

1 Maize grains used in this investigation are sown in an agar gel. This holds them firmly in position and supplies sufficient water for germination. When preparing the gels, it is essential to use a purified agar, such as bacteriological agar, otherwise growths of micro-organisms may contaminate the plates. Mix 2.5 g agar powder to a slurry with cold water, and add two drops of household bleach. Add the slurry to 100 cm^3 boiling water. Boil the mixture until all the agar powder has dissolved. Place the maize grains in position while the agar is still molten. After the plates have cooled and hardened, cut away part of each plate, immediately above the maize grains, as shown in Figure 28.

Fig. 28 *Sowing maize grains in agar*

(i) Place four, dry maize-grains in a row across the widest part of the dish. Turn the grains so that the embryo is facing upwards.

(ii) Pour hot, molten agar around the grains, to a depth of 2–4 mm. Allow the agar to cool and harden.

(iii) Use a sharp knife or scalpel to cut away the gel immediately above the maize grains.

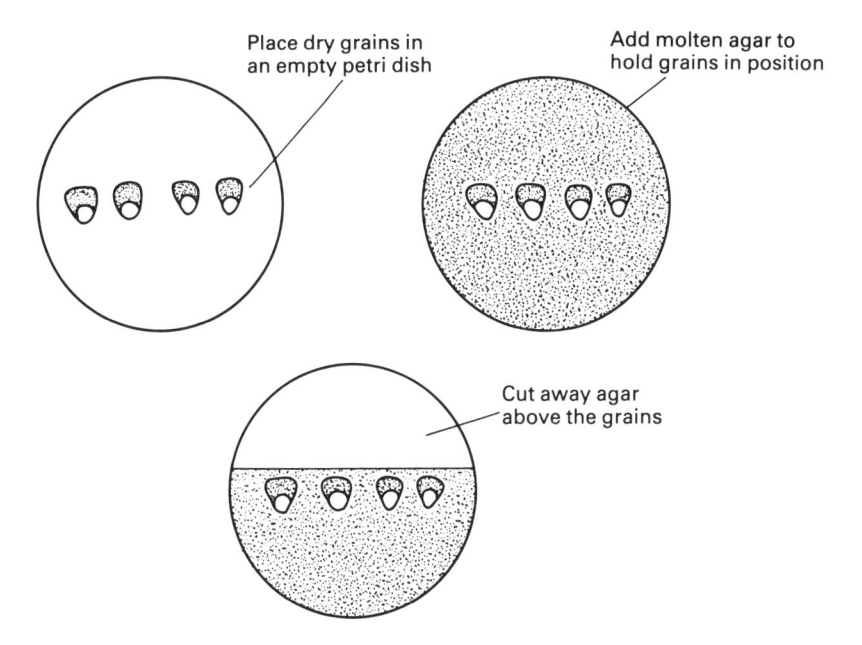

2 The agar plates should be prepared 7–10 days before the investigation.

Answers

	Marks
1 (a) Radicle.	1
(b) Downwards.	1
(c) Day 3.	1
2 (a) Plumule.	1
(b) Upwards.	1
(c) Day 5.	1
(d) Gravity.	1
3 (a) See Table 31.	2
(b) The root did not grow at a uniform rate. There was a daily increase in the rate of growth during the period from day 4–6.	2
4 (a) See Table 32.	2
(b) Growth of the young shoot was slower and more uniform than growth of the young root.	1
(c) The root lengthened rapidly at first to anchor the seedling to the soil, and to absorb water and mineral salts. Once the root had anchored the seedling, the shoot began to lengthen.	2

Table 31

Day	4	5	6
Increase in length (mm)	4	7	10

Table 32

Day	5	6	7
Increase in length (mm)	2	2	3

5 Ink marks just behind the root cap became more widely spaced. Other ink marks remained spaced at 2 mm apart. This shows that increase in length occurs in the region behind the root tip, not at the tip, nor uniformly along the length of the root.	2
6 The root bent. Bending occurred in the same region as increase in length. The upper and lower parts of this region grew at different rates, enabling the plant to respond to gravity.	2

29 Tropic responses and auxin production

TIME
Preparation: 15–20 minutes
Observation: 7–10 days
Investigation: 30–40 minutes

Skills tested: 5, 6, 7, 8, 16.

Materials

Preparation

■ Thirty barley grains ■ Petri dish, containing four or more germinating maize grains ■ Shoe box ■ Three petri dish bases ■ Small flower pot, or adhesive tape ■ Tissue paper ■ Electric lamp, fitted with a 60 W bulb ■ Scissors ■ Ruler, graduated in millimetres ■ Hand lens ■ Scalpel ■ Pencil ■ Glass-marking pen

Instructions and notes

1 Petri dishes, each containing from 6–8 maize grains in agar, should be prepared 12–15 days before the assessment (see Figure 32). After the grains have been sown, plates should be placed in a vertical position for 2–5 days, until plumules have reached a length of about 1 cm. Other materials for this investigation should be prepared 7–10 days before the assessment.
2 Sharp scalpels must be provided if pupils are to remove one-half of the tips of maize plumules.

Pupils should be warned that the scalpels are sharp.

Answers

Part A   **Marks**

1 (a) Dishes 1 and 3.   1
   (b) Dish 2.   1
2 Dish 2.   1

3 (a) Seedlings in dish 2 were green; those in dishes 1 and 3 were white/yellow. 1
  (b) The green pigment (chlorophyll) has developed in response to higher light intensity. The green pigment (chlorophyll) has developed in response to uniform illumination. 2
4 (a) They have curved shoots. 1
  (b) The shoots have bent in response to the light source. 2
  (c) Shoots grow towards light, which is essential for photosynthesis. 1
5 (a) Shoots grow most rapidly in darkness. 1
  (b) The dark side. 1
  (c) Growth is uniform. The shoot is straight. 1

Part B

6 (a) The uncut shoot. 1
  (b) The rate of growth is decreased. 1
  (c) The tip produces a growth-stimulating substance (auxin). 1
  (d) The shoot bends in the direction of the cut. 2
  (e) Only the intact half-tip produces a growth-stimulating substance (auxin). The net result is growth on the intact side, with bending in the direction of the cut. 2

30 Differences between seeds and seedlings

TIME
Investigation: 30–40 minutes

Skills tested: 1, 2, 3, 5, 6.

Materials

- Two soaked seeds of French bean, labelled A ■ Two soaked maize grains, labelled B ■ Seedling of French bean, labelled C ■ Seedling of maize, labelled D ■ Hand lens ■ Forceps ■ Scalpel

Instructions and notes

1 Seeds of French bean and fruits of maize should be soaked in water for 24 hours before they are distributed.

2 Seedlings of French bean and maize, each bearing two green leaves, should be grown by sowing seeds in moist vermiculite, peat or sawdust 7–10 days before they are required. The seedlings of French bean should be supplied with the cotyledons attached.
3 Specimens may be presented to pupils in a single petri dish, sub-divided into four labelled segments.

Answers

	Marks
1 See Figure 29.	3
2 See Figure 30.	5
3 See Figure 31.	6

4 The two cotyledons of French bean are raised above the soil surface (epigeal germination), whereas the single cotyledon of the maize remains below the soil surface (hypogeal germination).   2
Foliage leaves of the French bean are broad and net-veined, while those of the maize are narrow and parallel-veined.   2
5 (a) Storage of food.   1
   (b) Production of food by photosynthesis.   1

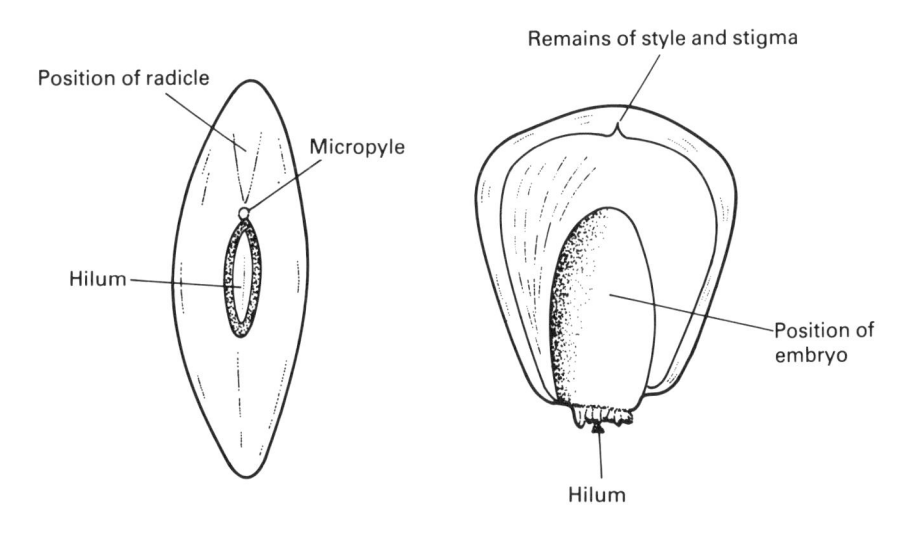

Fig. 29 *External appearance of the seeds*

(i) Bean seed   *(ii) Maize grain*

Labels for bean seed: Position of radicle, Micropyle, Hilum

Labels for maize grain: Remains of style and stigma, Position of embryo, Hilum

Fig. 30 *Internal appearance of the seeds*

(i) Bean seed

(ii) Maize grain

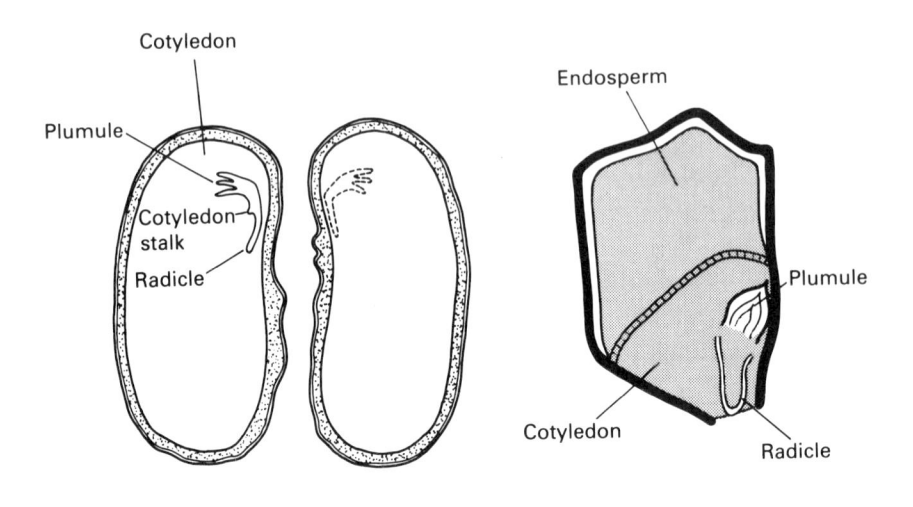

Fig. 31 *Seedlings of French bean and maize*

(i) French bean seedling

(ii) Maize seedling

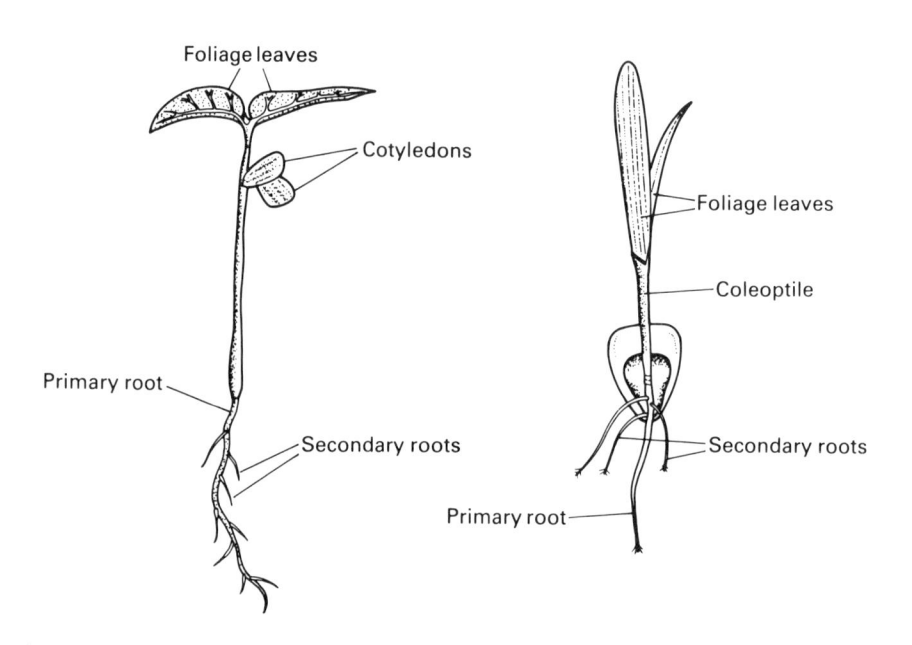

31 Adaptation: form and function in plant stems

TIME
Investigation: 30–40 minutes
November–April

Skills tested: 1, 3, 5, 6, 25.

Materials

Investigation

■ Woody deciduous twig, labelled A ■ Brussels sprout, labelled B ■ Potato, labelled C ■ Hand lens ■ Scalpel

Instructions and notes

1 Specimen A is a leafless, woody twig, such as lime, beech, or oak. It should have a terminal bud and several axillary buds.

Answers

Marks

1 See Figure 32. 4

Fig. 32 *Specimen A: woody twig of time*

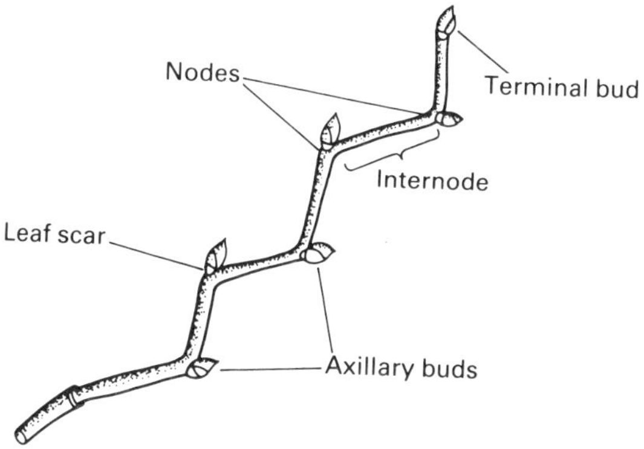
Nodes
Terminal bud
Internode
Leaf scar
Axillary buds

2 See Figure 33. 4

Fig. 33 *Specimen B: brussels sprout*

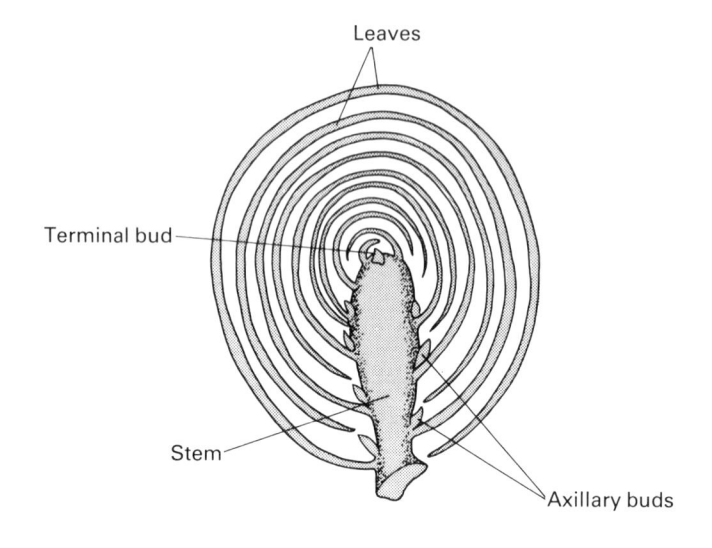

3 Specimens A and B are both stems, with a terminal bud, axillary buds, nodes, and internodes. 2
4 Leaves have fallen from specimen A, but are retained by specimen B. Specimen A has longer and fewer internodes than specimen B. In specimen A, the stem and buds are exposed, whereas in specimen B they are surrounded and protected by leaves. 4
5 (a) Stem. 1
  (b) The potato has a terminal bud and axillary buds. Ridges below the axillary buds are nodes. 2
6 The three specimens, although superficially very different in appearance, are all stems with similar structural features. They illustrate how a part of an organism, such as a stem, can evolve to assume different forms and perform different functions. 3

32 Behaviour of the woodlouse

TIME
Investigation: 30–40 minutes

Skills tested: 4, 5, 6, 9.

Materials

■ Four living woodlice in a stoppered boiling tube ■ Plastic petri dish ■ Protractor ■ Black paper/plastic sheet ■ Calcium chloride or silica gel, in a piece of nylon tights ■ Bench lamp, fitted with a 60 W bulb ■ Moist cotton wool ■ Elastic band ■ Forceps ■ Hand lens ■ Glass-marking pen

Instructions and notes

1 Wrap 3–4 pieces of calcium chloride or silica gel in a piece of nylon tights, or muslin, approximately 4 × 4 cm. Tie the ends with thread, or fasten them with a staple.
2 The black paper/plastic sheet should be large enough to form a sleeve, covering one-half of the boiling tube.
3 Keeping the woodlice in a dry, dark place for 1–2 hours before the experiment usually ensures that they make a rapid response to light and water. Any tin may be used for this purpose.

Answers

Marks

1 (a) See Figure 34.   2

Fig. 34 *Dorsal view of woodlouse* (Oniscus sp.)

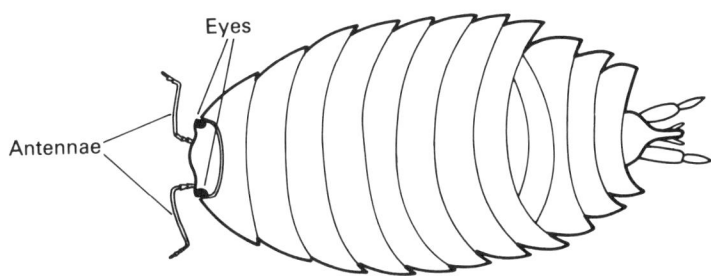

(b) Eye: light.
       Antennae: touch, contact, chemical stimuli, moisture. 2
2 (a) The woodlice moved into the darkened-half of the tube and remained in that half. 1
   (b) Negative phototaxis. 1
   (c) When they shelter in dark places the woodlice are hidden from predators that are active by day. Dark places are cooler and moister than those exposed to bright sunlight. 2
3 (a) If moist cotton wool had been put at the bottom of the tube, the sides may have been wetted. This would have prevented the formation of a moisture gradient. 1
   (b) Woodlice moved into the wet half. 1
   (c) Positive hydrotaxis. 1
4 (a) The woodlice moved towards the edge of the dish, and then began to move around the edge, keeping in contact with the side wall. 2
   (b) Heat and light from the lamp. 2
   (c) When in contact with the side wall of the dish, the woodlice reduced the area of their body surface exposed to the air. As a result, less water was lost to the atmosphere. 2
5 See Figure 35. 3

Fig. 35 *Arrangement of appartus to determine if a woodlouse can ascend a 20° slope*

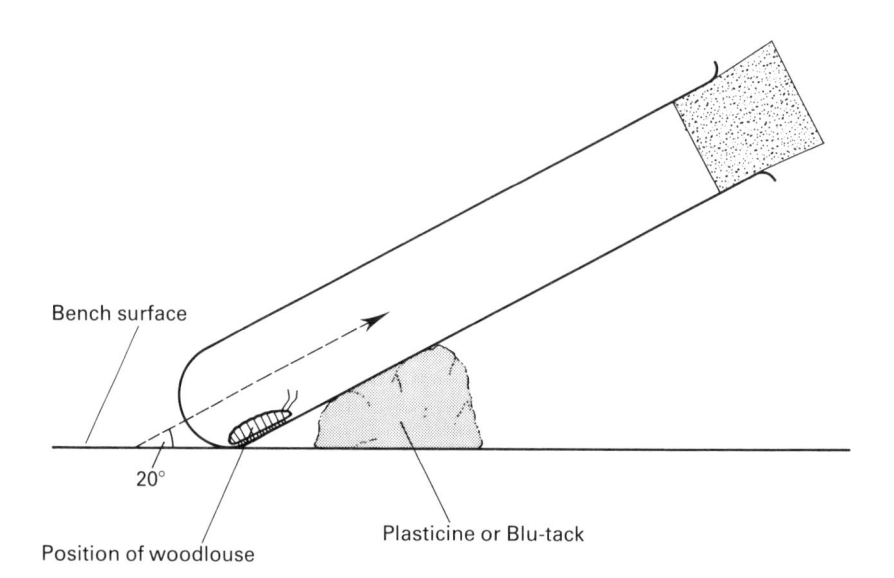

33 Body size in mammals

TIME
Investigation: 50–60 minutes

Skills tested: 5, 6, 7, 8, 13, 14, 16, 18.

Materials

- T.S. limb bone of sheep or pig ■ 500 cm³ beaker ■ 250 cm³ beaker ■ 100 cm³ beaker ■ Two thermometers ■ Six sheets of A4 or foolscap paper ■ Packets of exercise books (or alternative means of loading) ■ Bunsen burner, tripod and gauze ■ Ruler ■ Scissors ■ Adhesive tape ■ Graph paper

Instructions and notes

1 Limb bones are available from butchers. They may be held in a vice and sawn transversely into lengths of 1.0–1.5 cm. A hacksaw or tenon saw should be used.
2 A large number of books of uniform size, such as exercise books, should be available to pupils. A plastic bucket, filled with dry sand or brass weights could provide an alternative system for loading. The bucket should be supported on a piece of cardboard or hardboard.
3 Pupils should be provided with glass beakers.

Answers

Part A   Marks

1 (a) See Table 33.   3

  (b) See Figure 36.   4
  (c) The 100 cm³ beaker.   1
  (d) The surface area:volume ratio is greater in the 100 cm³ beaker.   1
  (e) A baby. The surface area:volume ratio is greater in a baby than
      in an adult.   2

Part B

2 (a) The long paper cylinders supported 27 exercise books.   1
  (b) The short paper cylinders supported 38 exercise books.   1

(c) Long bones of the limbs. 1
(d) Compression. 1
(e) Short, broad cylinders. 1
3 (a) Limb bones resemble hollow cylinders, with an outer ring of hard material that resists compression. 1
(b) It is harder and more rigid, with soft material at the centre. 1
4 Overweight people lower their surface area:volume ratio. Therefore, they lose heat less rapidly and tend to become overheated. The additional mass that they carry slows their rate of movement, partly by increasing the force of compression on bones in the legs. 2

Table 33

| Time (minutes) | Temperature (°C) | |
	100 cm³ beaker	250 cm³ beaker
0	70	70
5	58	62
10	54	60
15	51	58
20	48	56
25	45	54
30	42	52

Fig. 36 *Rates of cooling in two beakers of hot water*

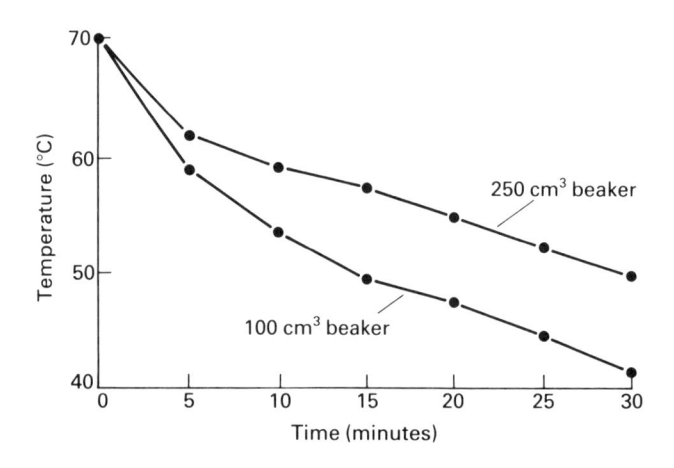

34 Exercise: measuring performance

TIME
Preparation: 30–40 minutes
Investigation: 30–40 minutes

Skills tested: 5, 6, 7, 9, 10, 13, 14, 15, 16.

Materials

Preparation

- Gymnasium bench ■ Metronome ■ Five stop-watches ■ Wrist-watch

Investigation

- Record of results ■ Graph paper

Instructions and notes

1 Exercises may be carried out at any time before the investigation is given. The aim, of course, is to collect data for analysis.

> **If these exercises are carried out by pupils, it is important that they should be properly supervised. Pupils should be warned against straining, and any who are known to suffer from defects of the cardiovascular, renal or muscular systems should not participate.**

Answers

Part A
Marks

1 (a) See Table 34.   2
  (b) See Figure 37.   2
  (c) The fastest part of the run was from 40–60 metres.   1
  (d) $20 \times \frac{60}{2.3} \times 60 = 31{,}320$ metres per hour.   2

Table 34

Distance (m)	Time (s)	Time over each 20 m distance (s)
20	3.1	3.1
40	6.0	2.9
60	8.3	2.3
80	11.4	3.1
100	15.4	4.0

Fig. 37 *Time taken to run each 20 m stretch of a 100 m race*

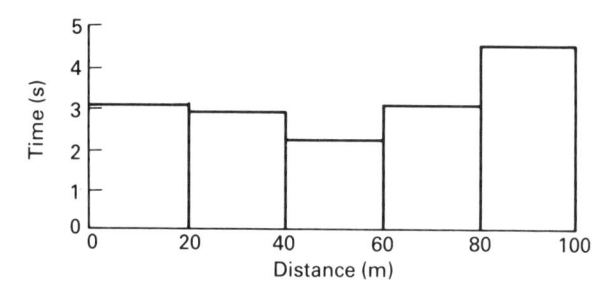

Part B

2 (a) See Figure 38. 4

Fig. 38 *Effect of exercise on the rate of heartbeat*

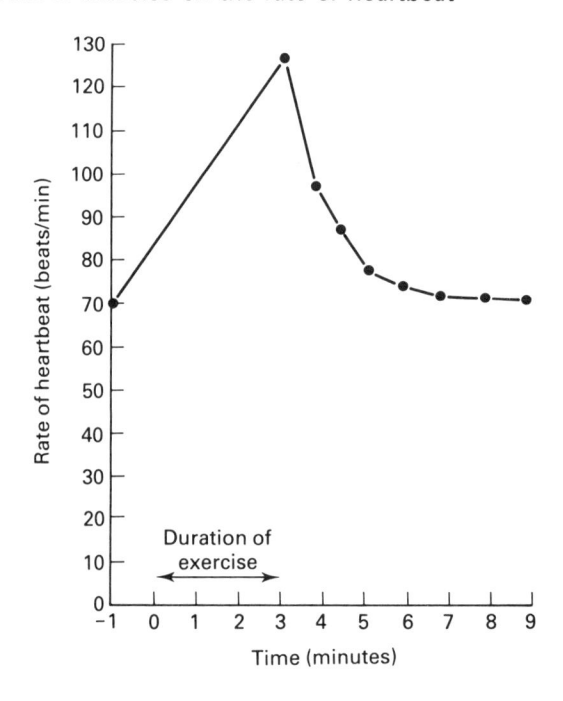

(b) The faster the rate of heartbeat, the harder the heart is working to pump blood to the tissues. 1

(c) (i) A slower heartbeat indicates that the efficiency of the heart has improved. 1

(ii) A faster heartbeat indicates reduced efficiency of the heart. The heart has to work harder in order to pump a similar amount of blood to the tissues. 1

Part C

3 Measure the distance from a person's knee to the floor. Subdivide this distance into 10 units of equal length. Mark-off and number these units on a metre rule, or on the leg itself. (Mark 1 is at the knee; mark 10 is at floor level.) Ask the person to stand up and bend forward as far as possible, in an attempt to place the palms of the hands on the ground. Relate the level of the wrist to the mark immediately above it. The number of this mark is the score recorded. 6

35 Carbon dioxide in inspired and expired air

TIME
Investigation: 30–40 minutes

Skills tested: 5, 6, 7, 8, 13, 15, 16, 18, 20.

Materials

- Apparatus as shown in Figure 38
- Three test tubes in a rack
- O 15 cm³ hydrogen carbonate (bicarbonate) indicator solution
- 5 cm³ dilute hydrochloric acid
- 5 cm³ dilute sodium hydroxide solution
- 5 cm³ plastic syringe
- 20 cm glass tube
- Stop-clock, or watch with a second hand
- Glass-marking pen
- Safety spectacles

Instructions and notes

1 Prepare hydrogen carbonate (bicarbonate) indicator by dissolving 0.84 g Analar sodium hydrogen carbonate in 500 cm³ distilled water, and then make up the final volume to 1 dm³ with distilled water. Add to this a solution of 0.1 g cresol-red and 0.2 g thymol-blue, dissolved in 20 cm³ ethanol.

On the day of the assessment, dilute the indicator with nine times its own volume of distilled water. Add just enough dilute sodium hydroxide solution to make the indicator purple-red.

71

2 Construct each piece of apparatus from two boiling tubes, two rubber bungs, glass tubing and rubber tubing, ensuring that the apparatus is airtight when the bungs are in position. Put approximately 5 cm^3 hydrogen carbonate (bicarbonate) indicator solution into each tube. See Figure 39.

Fig. 39 *Apparatus for comparing the amounts of carbon dioxide in inspired and expired air*

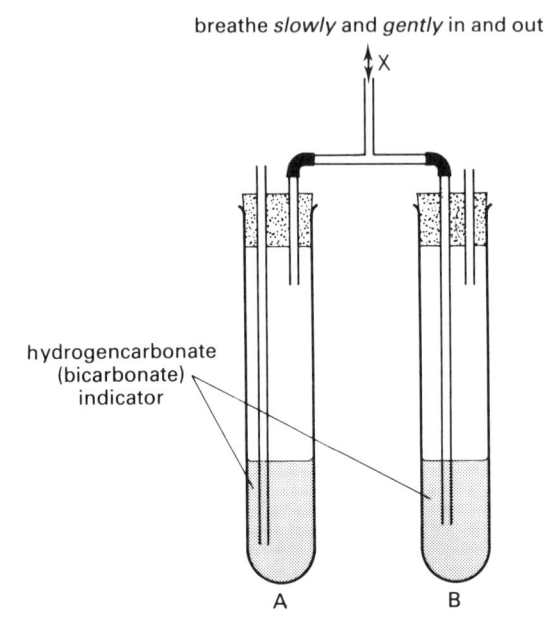

Answers

	Marks
2 The indicator changed colour, through yellow to pink-red.	1
3 The indicator changed colour from red-purple to blue-purple.	1
4 (a) The indicator became yellow.	1
(b) Expired air contains a soluble gas that is acid.	1
(c) Carbon dioxide.	1
5 (a) Tube A.	1
(b) Tube B.	1
6 (a) See Table 35.	2

Table 35

Tube	A	B
Time for colour change (s)	280	20

(b) Both inspired and expired air contains carbon dioxide, which dissolves in the indicator solution, forming an acid (yellow colour). There is more carbon dioxide in expired air than in inspired air, hence the indicator changes colour more rapidly in tube B than in tube A. 4

7 $0.03 \times \dfrac{\text{Time (s) for colour change in inspired air}}{\text{Time (s) for colour change in expired air}}$ 2

8 (a) (i) There would be no difference in the rate of colour change. 1
 (ii) The rate of colour change would increase. 1
 (b) There is no change in the amount of carbon dioxide in the inspired air passing through tube A. In expired air, passing through tube B, the amount of carbon dioxide has increased, as a result of the breakdown of additional carbohydrate (glucose) during exercise. 3

36 Fermentation of glucose by yeast

TIME
Preparation: 15–20 minutes
Observation: 60–80 minutes
Investigation: 30–40 minutes

Skills tested: 5, 6, 7, 8, 13, 14, 15, 16.

Materials

Preparation

- 10 cm^3 suspension of yeast cells ■ 10 cm^3 glucose solution ■ 5 cm^3 ethanol ■ Two 100 cm^3 beakers ■ Two 10 cm^3 plastic syringes ■ Two 30 cm lengths of capillary tubing ■ Two short lengths of rubber tubing ■ Retort stand, boss and clamp ■ Clock, or watch ■ Ruler, graduated in millimetres ■ Glass-marking pen

Investigation

- Record of results ■ Graph paper

Instructions and notes

1. The suspension of yeast cells is prepared by adding 10 g dried yeast to 10 cm^3 water. The yeast should be activated by adding a little sugar to the suspension, and allowing it to stand for a few hours, or overnight.
2. The solution of glucose is prepared by dissolving 10 g in 100 cm^3 water.
3. The suspensions of yeast cells, glucose solution, and ethanol or water should be prepared about 90 minutes before the investigation, then observed continuously for a period of 60–80 minutes. There is often a delay of 30–45 minutes before yeast cells begin to ferment glucose.

> Lengths of capillary tubing should be flame-polished at both ends to remove any sharp projections.

Answers

Marks

1 See Table 36.

Table 36

Time (min)	Length of column in capillary tube (cm)	
	Syringe 1	Syringe 2
0	0	0
10	0	0
20	0	0
30	0	0
40	3	1
50	10	2
60	23	2
70	38	2

2 See Figure 40.   8
3 (a) Syringe 1.   1
   (b) Ethanol acted as an inhibitor, reducing the rate of respiration.   1
4 Respiration was mostly anaerobic. The only point at which oxygen could reach the cells was via the capillary tubing.   2

5 $\dfrac{5}{15} \times 100 = 33.3\%$ 2

6 Carbon dioxide, produced as an end product of anaerobic respiration, displaces an equivalent volume of mixture. The only direction in which displacement can occur is along the capillary tubing.   2

Fig. 40 *Effect of ethanol on the rate of glucose fermentation by yeast*

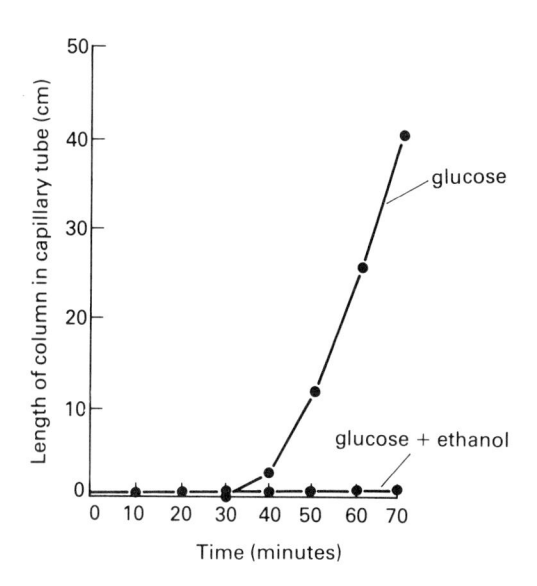

37 Making use of yeast

TIME
Preparation: 10–15 minutes
Observation: 7 days
Investigation: 60–80 minutes

Skills tested: 5, 6, 7, 8, 13, 14, 15, 16.

Materials

Preparation

- 5 g dried yeast ■ 150 cm^3 sucrose solution ■ 100 cm^3 measuring cylinder ■ Winemaker's plastic hydrometer ■ Jam jar, or similar container ■ Cotton wool

Investigation

- 50 cm^3 dough, in a beaker ■ 100 cm^3 measuring cylinder ■ 1 dm^3 beaker ■ Thermometer ■ Bunsen burner, tripod and gauze ■ Clock, or watch ■ Record of results ■ Graph paper

Instructions and notes

1. The sucrose solution contains 10 g dissolved in 100 cm^3 water.
2. A suitable dough, which rises rapidly, may be prepared by blending the following materials to a smooth paste: 50 g plain flour, 20 g caster sugar, 5 g dried yeast, 100 cm^3 water.
3. That part of the investigation involving measurements of specific gravity should be set up 7 days before the investigation. Plastic hydrometers are available from stores that supply materials for home wine-making.

Answers

Part A   Marks
2 See Table 37.   2

Table 37

Time (mins)	0	5	10	15	20	25	30	35	40	45
Volume of dough (cm^3)	30	31	34	39	46	48	45	45	45	45

3 See Figure 40.   4
4 (a) The curve is S-shaped until the dough collapses, then flat.   1
  (b) $\frac{18}{30} \times 100 = 60\%$ 2
  (c) The dough stops rising when the 'skin' of flour breaks, and bubbles of gas escape from the dough into the atmosphere. 2

Part B

5 See Table 38.   4
6 Six days.   1
7 (a) Other organisms, including bacteria, may get into the sugar solution, spoil the flavour of the beer or wine, or even produce substances that are harmful if taken internally. 2
  (b) Carbon dioxide produced during fermentation must be able to escape to the atmosphere. If it is retained in a glass vessel, internal pressure may build up to a level that causes glass to shatter. This could cause injury. Plastic containers are shatter-proof, and air locks allow gas to escape, without admitting micro-organisms from the air. 2

Fig. 41 *Expansion of dough*

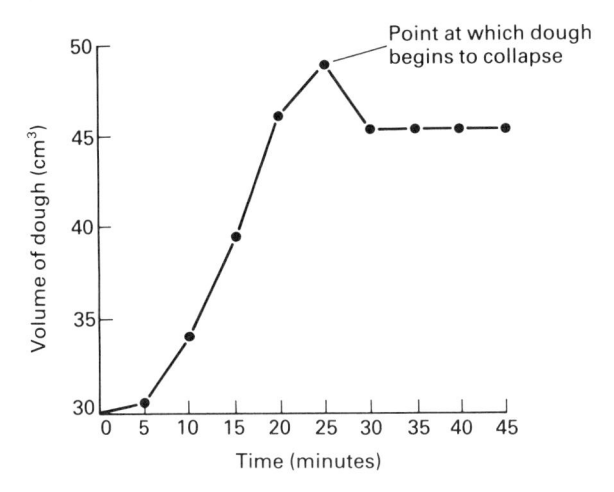

[Graph: Volume of dough (cm³) vs Time (minutes), showing dough volume rising from 30 at 5 min to ~49 at 25 min (Point at which dough begins to collapse), then dropping to ~45.5 and levelling off through 45 min.]

Table 38

Time (days)	0	1	2	3	4	5	6	7
Specific gravity (S. G.)	1.036	1.032	1.022	1.010	1.002	1.000	0.098	0.098

38 The effects of a selective weedkiller on a lawn

TIME
Preparation: 30 minutes, and 30 minutes after 2–3 weeks
Investigation: 30–40 minutes
April–September

Skills tested: 5, 6, 7, 8, 12, 13, 15, 16, 23.

Materials

Preparation

Part 1 ■ Selective weedkiller ■ Metre quadrat ■ Watering can, fitted with a fine rose ■ Hammer ■ Wooden pegs ■ Illustrated guide to the British flora

77

Part 2 ■ Metre quadrat

Investigation

■ Record of results

Instructions and notes

1 Plants on which the investigation is to be carried out, should be identified from an illustrated guide to the British flora. Suitable guides are listed on page 102.
2 The selective weedkiller should be prepared according to the manufacturer's instructions. Select a site for study that is accessible at all times, but not subject to mowing or other interference during the period of the investigation. It is suggested that the teacher should apply the weedkiller, again following the manufacturer's instructions.

Answers

	Marks
1 See Table 39.	6

Table 39

Condition of lawn	Grass	Cover value 'Rosette' plant	'Creeping' plant
Before applying weedkiller	100	87	97
After applying weedkiller	100	3	9

2 (a) $\frac{0}{100} \times 100 = 0\%$ 2

(b) $\frac{84}{87} \times 100 = 96.5\%$ 2

(c) $\frac{88}{97} \times 100 = 90.0\%$ 2

3 (a) The 'rosette' plant. 1
  (b) Grass. 1

4 Selective weedkillers would kill most flowers and vegetables, as these are broad-leaved species. 2
5 Selective weedkillers are persistent. Even after composting, enough weedkiller may remain in the compost to affect the growth of flowers and vegetables, if the compost was applied to garden soil. 2
6 Several quadrats should have been applied to the lawn to increase the size of the sample. More than one 'rosette' plant and 'creeping' plant should have been included in the investigation. 2

39 The effects of artificial fertiliser on a population of water plants

TIME
Preparation: 5–15 minutes
Observation: 6–10 weeks
Investigation: 40–50 minutes
May–September

Skills tested: 5, 6, 7, 8, 13, 22.

Materials

Preparation

- Duckweed plants
- Two 250 cm^3 beakers
- Artificial fertiliser
- Glass-marking pen

Investigation

- Two populations of duckweed plants, in 250 cm^3 beakers
- Individual records of population growth
- Graph paper

Instructions and notes

1 It is best to use a granular form of artificial fertiliser, available from garden centres.
2 This is a long-term investigation that pupils could carry out in school or at home. Each pupil will require approximately 100 cm^2 bench-space in a greenhouse. Alternatively, each beaker may be put into a polythene bag. After tying with string, the bags can be placed out-of-doors in a suitable

position. The investigation should be terminated only after population growth is complete. This may take from 6–10 weeks, depending on climatic conditions.

Answers

Marks

1 See Table 40.   3

Table 40

Weeks	No. duckweed plants	
	No fertiliser	Fertiliser added
0	4	4
1	6	12
2	18	34
3	29	72
4	38	94
5	40	120
6	43	125
7	46	128
8	48	129

2 See Figure 42.   5

Fig. 42 *Growth of duckweed populations*

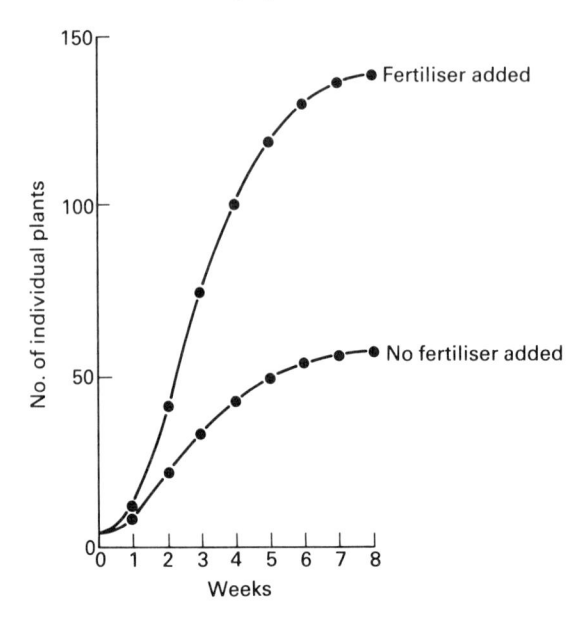

3 It is important to make counts at regular intervals of time if accurate results are to be obtained. 2
4 (a) Artificial fertiliser increased the rate of population growth. 1
  (b) The fertiliser provided plant food, in the form of mineral salts, essential for the formation and growth of new plants. 1
5 All available space was occupied. Mineral salts were used up. The plants produced waste products that prevented further increases in numbers. 1
6 (a) After 5–6 weeks it was difficult to make accurate counts of the large number of plants in each beaker. 1
  (b) Count plants in one-half, or one-quarter of the beaker, and calculate total numbers. Start with a single plant and grow it in a smaller beaker of water. 1
7 Water in the beaker containing fertiliser was green, following the growth of microscopic algae. Artificial fertiliser, washed from fields into ponds and rivers, may cause a similar algal bloom. This would reduce the amount of light reaching other aquatic plants, by causing the water to become turbid. 2
8 Herbivores might gain an initial advantage from the rapid growth of green plants, but green algae could block the gills of fish and other aquatic animals. Moreover, when the algae died, and their bodies were decomposed by bacteria and fungi, the oxygen content of the water would fall. 3

40 Some characteristics of a population of trees

TIME
Preparation: 40–60 minutes
Investigation: 30–40 minutes

Skills tested: 5, 6, 7, 8, 11, 12, 13, 14, 15, 16, 18, 23.

Materials

Preparation

- 5 m tape measure, graduated in centimetres
- Copy of table, mounted on cardboard
- Pencil

Investigation

- Record of results
- Graph paper

Instructions and notes

1 As pupils work in pairs during this investigation, one tape measure is required per pair. Each pupil, however, should make their own record of results.
2 Teachers should help pupils identify oak, beech, and ivy from features of their leaves, twigs and bark.
3 Pupils will require access to a fairly large area of woodland, dominated either by oak or beech trees. Some of the older trees should be colonised by ivy.

Answers

Part A
Marks

1 See Figure 43.   6

Fig. 43 *Size distribution of oaks in mature oak woodland. Shaded portions indicate the number of trees in each group colonised by ivy*

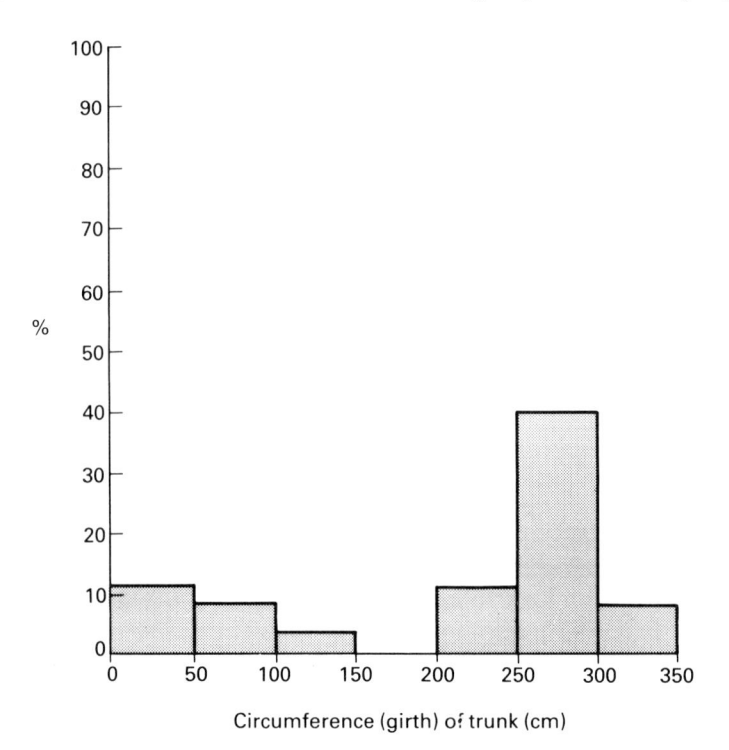

2 The wood contained trees of different sizes. Most of the trees were large, mature oaks that had dominated other vegetation for many years. Continuous shading by these mature trees had checked the growth of all but fairly small individuals. These younger trees had managed to become established in positions where some light penetrated through the leaf canopy 4
3 Breast-height differs markedly between pupils. A specific height, such as 1.3 m above ground level, would have been preferable. 2

Part B

4 See shaded portion of Figure 43. 4
5 Ivy may be absent from the trunks of young trees, but is almost always present on the trunks of large, mature individuals. 2
6 Ivy colonises trees from ground level, then grows up the trunk. The older the tree, the more likely it is to be colonised by ivy. 2

41 Finding the size of an animal population

TIME
Preparation: 30 minutes, and 30 minutes after 4–5 days
Investigation: 30–40 minutes
April–September

Skills tested: 4, 5, 6, 7, 13, 15, 16, 18, 23.

Materials

Preparation

- Slug pellets
- White cellulose paint
- Paint brush

Investigation

- Record of results
- Fifty marbles or beads
- White cellulose paint
- Paint brush
- Cocoa tin, or opaque container with a lid
- Table spoon
- Petri dish base

83

Instructions and notes

1 Attempts to estimate the size of a snail population should be made 4–5 days before the investigation. In areas where snails are uncommon, field studies may be attempted on populations of woodlice or grasshoppers.

Answers

	Marks
Part A	
1 See Table 41.	3

Table 41

No. snails marked (F_1)	20
No. snails captured, or killed, in the second sample (F_2)	10
No. marked snails in second sample (F_3)	6

2 $\dfrac{20 \times 10}{6} = 33.3$ — 2

3 $\dfrac{10 \times 100}{33} = 30.3\%$ — 2

4 $100 - 30.3 = 69.7\%$ — 2

Part B

5 $20 \times \dfrac{10}{3} = 66.6\%$ — 2

6 $20 \times \dfrac{10}{5} = 40\%$ and, $20 \times \dfrac{10}{6} = 33.3\%$ — 4

7 $\dfrac{66.6 + 40 + 33.3}{3} = 46.6\%$ — 2

8 $50.0 - 46.6 = 3.4$ — 1

9 The Lincoln index provides a fairly accurate estimate of population size if a large number of individuals in the population are marked and subsequently recaptured. If only a small number of marked individuals are recaptured, the estimates are likely to be inaccurate. — 2

42 Pollution of water and air

TIME
Preparation: 10–15 minutes and 15–20 minutes
Observation: 4 weeks
Investigation: 30–40 minutes
April–September

Skills tested: 5, 6, 7, 8, 13, 14, 15, 16, 22.

Materials

Preparation

Part 1 ■ Plants of duckweed ■ Three 1 dm^3 beakers, or Kilner jars ■ Glass-marking pen

Part 2 ■ Leaves of a known tree ■ Nutrient, or malt agar plate ■ Vaseline ■ Cork-borer (No. 7–10) ■ Incubator, kept at 35 °C ■ Glass-marking pen

Investigation

■ Record of results ■ Graph paper

Instructions and notes

1 Nutrient or malt agar should be prepared according to the manufacturer's instructions.
2 The majority of fungi on the surfaces of leaves are pink-coloured yeasts (*Sporobolomyces roseus*).

> After the fungal colonies have grown, and before they are inspected by pupils, each plate should be sealed with adhesive tape to prevent inhalation of fungal spores. At the end of the assessment the agar plates should be collected, placed in a heat-resistant bag, and incinerated. Water-samples should not be collected from any pond or river polluted by human effluents, notably sewage.

3 Each pupil will require approximately 200 cm² bench-space in a greenhouse. As an alternative, each beaker may be placed in a polythene bag. After blowing up the bag and tying it with string, it may be placed out of doors in a suitable position.
4 This investigation is prepared in two stages. The first stage, to test for water pollution, is set up four weeks before the investigation. The second stage, to test for air pollution, is set up two days before the investigation.

Answers

Marks

Part A

1 See Table 42. 3

Table 42

Weeks	No. duckweed plants		
	Distilled water	Tap water	Pond water
0	4	4	4
1	5	6	8
2	6	8	15
3	6	10	34
4	7	12	58

2 See Figure 44. 5

Fig. 44 *Growth of duckweed in three different samples of water*

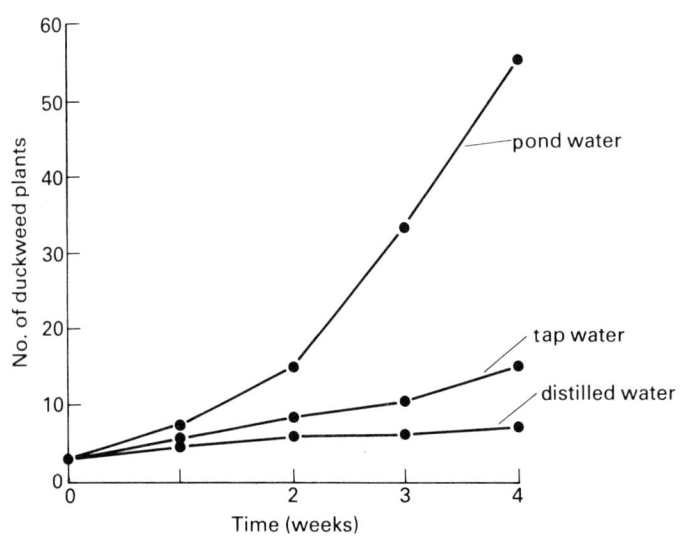

3 Growth of duckweed in pond water was faster than in tap water. This suggests that the pond water, taken from a pond near a farm, contained some pollutants, possibly farmyard manure, urine, or decomposing organic matter. 2

Part B

4 (a) See Table 43. 4

Table 43

Site of collection	No. fungal colonies		
	Disc 1	Disc 2	Disc 3
'Polluted' area	6	8	3
'Unpolluted' area	8	8	14

(b) Mean (average) No. colonies from 'polluted' area

$$= \frac{6+8+3}{3} = 5.6$$

Mean (average) No. colonies from 'unpolluted' area

$$2 = \frac{8+8+14}{3} = 10.0$$

(c) Results suggest that there are more fungi on leaves from the 'unpolluted' area, but larger samples would have to be taken to confirm this. Chemical compounds in smoke from factory chimneys or from car exhausts may reduce the number of fungi on leaf surfaces. 2

5 While the dish was standing on the bench, spores of the fungi were raining down from the discs on t the nutrient agar. This was stopped after 15 minutes. If it had continued, so many colonies would have grown that it would have been difficult to make counts. 2

43 Organic pollution of water samples

TIME
Investigation: 40–50 minutes

Skills tested: 5, 6, 7, 8, 9, 10, 13, 14, 15, 16, 22.

Materials

- 10 cm^3 pond water, in a beaker ■ 10 cm^3 tap water, in a beaker
- 5 cm^3 5-vol. hydrogen peroxide solution ■ Two 1 cm^3 plastic syringe
- Two 20 cm lengths of capillary tubing ■ Two 2 cm lengths of rubber tubing ■ Boss, clamp, and retort stand ■ Stop-clock, or watch with a second hand ■ Ruler, graduated in millimetres ■ Glass-marking pen ■ Plastic gloves ■ Safety spectacles ■ Graph paper

Instructions and notes

1 Glass capillary tubing, with a bore of 2.0 cm diameter, should be provided, together with rubber tubing of 2–4 mm diameter. Pupils require the rubber tubing to join the nozzle of each syringe to a capillary tube.

> **Pupils should wear safety spectacles and plastic gloves when handling hydrogen peroxide solution. They should be warned that hydrogen peroxide can burn and bleach the skin. Any spillages should be washed off with plenty of water.**

2 Water samples may be collected from a pond, river or rain-water tank.

> **Any water known to be polluted with human effluents should be avoided.**

Answers

	Marks
5 See Table 44.	4
6 See Figure 45	6

Table 44

Time (minutes)	Distance travelled by meniscus (cm³)	
	Tap water	Pond water
0	0.0	0.0
1	0.0	2.5
2	0.0	5.3
3	0.1	8.9
4	0.1	12.1
5	0.2	15.9

Fig. 45 *Breakdown of hydrogen peroxide by tap water and pond water*

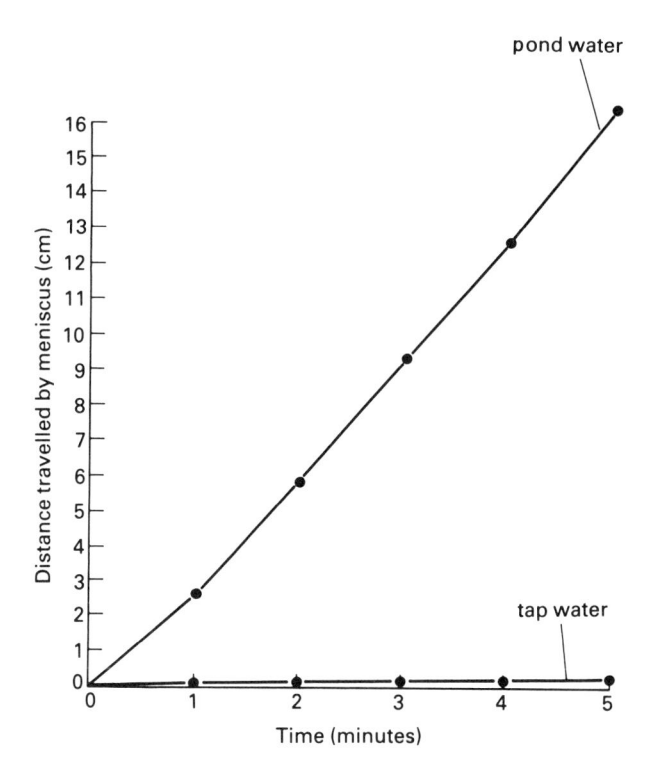

7 Pond water breaks down hydrogen peroxide solution more rapidly than tap water. An enzyme (catalase) produced by micro-organisms in the pond water is responsible for the increased rate of breakdown. Determining the rate at which oxygen is liberated provides an indirect method of comparing numbers of micro-organisms in water samples.   3

8 Collect two samples of pond water, one from the top and the other from the bottom of a pond. Prepare 5 vol. hydrogen peroxide solution. Draw 0.5 cm^3 water from the top of the pond into a 1 cm^3 plastic syringe, and 0.5 cm^3 wate from the bottom of the pond into a second 1 cm^3 syringe. Draw 0.5 cm^3 hydrogen peroxide solution into each tube. Mix the contents. After fitting rubber tubing and a capillary tube to each syringe, support the syringes with a clamp. Apply gentle pressure to the handle of each syringe to obtain a meniscus at the top of each tube. At intervals of 1 minute, over a period of 5 minutes, mark the position of the meniscus in each tube. Measure the distances and plot a graph of the results. 7

(The water sample that breaks down hydrogen peroxide most rapidly, and causes most rapid movement of the meniscus, is the one that contains most organic material.)

44 Water retention by sand, loam and peat soils

TIME
Investigation: 30–40 minutes

Skills tested: 5, 6, 7, 8, 11, 12, 13, 15, 16.

Materials

- 750 g coarse sand, labelled A ■ 750 g loam, labelled B ■ 750 g peat, labelled C ■ Three plastic flower pots (to rest inside 250 cm^3 beakers) ■ Three 250 cm^3 beakers ■ 200 cm^3 beaker ■ 100 cm^3 plastic measuring cylinder ■ Glass-marking pen

Instructions and notes

1 John Innes potting compost No. 3 is a suitable loam soil. This, together with coarse sand and peat, may be purchased from garden centres. The sand and loam should be dried in an oven at 100–150 °C before they are given to pupils. The peat should be moistened. Approximately 24 hours before the investigation, half fill a bucket with peat, pour a kettle of boiling water over it, and leave it overnight. Squeeze as much water as possible from the peat before it is distributed.

Answers

Part A

			Marks
2	(a)	Sand.	1
	(b)	Loam.	1
3	(a)	See Table 45.	6

(b) $\dfrac{64}{100} \times 100 = 64\,\%$ 2

(c) Soil samples should have been weighed, not measured by volume. Peat, like the sand and loam, should have been dried before the investigation.   2

Part B

4 (a) Results should fall within the limits shown in Table 46 below.   4

(b) The depth of each type of soil particle was read-off from the scale on the measuring cylinder, and the figures were doubled.   2

(c) Clay and humus.   2

Table 45

Soil	Sand (A)	Loam (B)	Peat (C)
Volume of water collected in beaker (cm³)	58	36	48
Volume of water retained by soil (cm³)	42	64	52

Table 46

Type of soil particle	% composition
Humus	8–15
Clay	10–25
Sand	60–75
Gravel	10–20

45 Soil pH

TIME
Investigation: 60–90 minutes

Skills tested: 5, 6, 7, 13, 14, 15, 16.

Materials

- 50 g garden top-soil, in a 250 cm^3 beaker ■ 2 g peat ■ 2 g loam
- 2 g lime ■ 50 cm^3 urea solution ■ 25 cm^3 distilled water
- Universal indicator (2) ■ Universal indicator chart (2) ■ Five test tubes ■ Narrow range pH 6.0–8.0 papers (2) ■ Glass rod ■ Spatula
- Forceps ■ Glass-marking pen ■ Graph paper

Instructions and notes

1 The urea solution contains 10 g dissolved in 100 cm^3 water.
2 Universal indicator may be diluted with ten times its own volume of distilled water to produce a suitable colour indicator for soil testing.
3 Top-soil from a vegetable garden, especially one that has been dressed with farmyard manure, is usually a good source of urease.

Answers

Marks

1 See Table 47. 2

Table 47

Time (minutes)	0	10	20	30	40	50	60
pH	6.0	6.5	7.0	7.5	7.5	8.0	8.5

2 See Figure 46. 4
3 The soil might become very alkaline, and this would have an adverse effect on crops. 1

Fig. 46 *Changes in the pH of a soil after adding urea*

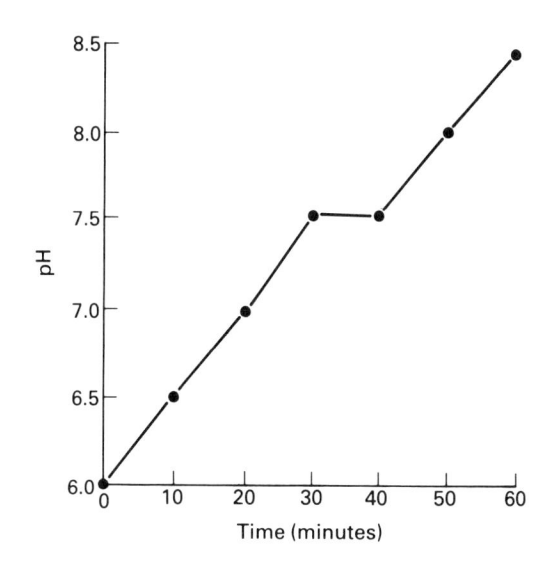

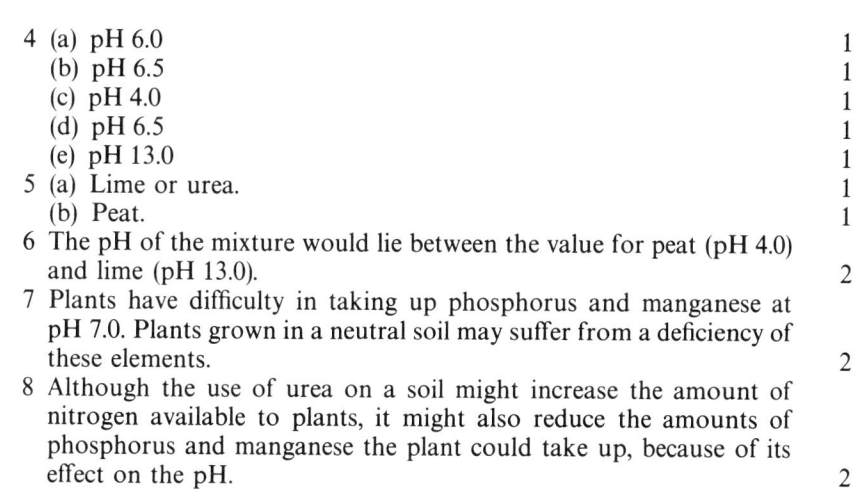

4 (a) pH 6.0   1
  (b) pH 6.5   1
  (c) pH 4.0   1
  (d) pH 6.5   1
  (e) pH 13.0   1
5 (a) Lime or urea.   1
  (b) Peat.   1
6 The pH of the mixture would lie between the value for peat (pH 4.0) and lime (pH 13.0).   2
7 Plants have difficulty in taking up phosphorus and manganese at pH 7.0. Plants grown in a neutral soil may suffer from a deficiency of these elements.   2
8 Although the use of urea on a soil might increase the amount of nitrogen available to plants, it might also reduce the amounts of phosphorus and manganese the plant could take up, because of its effect on the pH.   2

46 Organic matter in soil

TIME
Preparation: 5–10 minutes
Investigation: 60–90 minutes

Skills tested: 5, 6, 7, 8, 11, 12, 13, 15, 16, 18, 20.

Materials

Preparation

- Two polythene bags ■ Spade or garden trowel ■ Pestle and mortar
- Incubator or oven, kept at 35 °C ■ Glass-marking pen

Investigation

■ 70 g top-soil ■ 70 g sub-soil ■ 100 cm^3 sucrose solution ■ Two 100 cm^3 beakers ■ Eight Clinistix reagent strips (2, 3) ■ Two glass rods ■ Two metal sand trays ■ Tongs ■ Bunsen burner and tripod ■ Spatula ■ Top-pan balance ■ Aluminium foil ■ Glass-marking pen ■ Safety spectacles

Instructions and notes

1. The sucrose solution contains 10 g dissolved in 100 cm^3 water.
2. Each Clinistix reagent strip may be cut longitudinally into two halves.
3. Soil samples should be dug at least one day before the investigation. If possible, they should be taken from a garden to which leaf mould, or compost has been applied.

> **Pupils should wear safety spectacles when heating soil on a sand tray. There is a possibility of eye injury from hot ash when the soil is turned.**

Answers

                                                                                    Marks

1. (a) See Table 48.   2
   (b) Top-soil, which contains more organic matter than sub-soil, also
       has a higher level of invertase activity. Therefore, there appears to
       be a positive relationship between amounts of organic matter in a
       soil and its invertase activity.   3
3. (a) Organic matter was burned; that is, converted into gases and ash.   1
   (b) Nothing happened to the inorganic matter, as it is inert.   1
4. See Table 49.   4
5. (a) $\dfrac{2.5}{20} \times 100 = 12.5\%$ organic matter.   2
   (b) $\dfrac{0.5}{20} \times 100 = 2.5\%$ organic matter.   2
6. It is unlikely that all of the organic matter is burned after only 5–10
   minutes of heating.
   Ash from burned organic matter remains in the soil. This fraction of
   the organic matter is not lost during heating. The soil may still contain
   some water, which would be lost during heating.   3
7. Prepare samples of soil from the victim's boots and suspect's garden.
   Heat samples of each soil and find the amounts of organic matter they
   contained. Apply the test for invertase activity to both samples. If
   similar results were obtained from both samples, they could have had
   the same origin.   2

Table 48

Time (minutes)	Concentration of glucose (g/100 cm^3)	
	Top-soil	Sub-soil
0	0	0
15	0.25	0
30	0.5	0
45	0.75	0

Table 49

	Top-soil	Sub-soil
Mass before testing (g)	20	20
Mass after heating (g)	17.5	19.5
Mass of organic matter (g)	2.5	0.5

47 Decomposers in the soil

TIME
Preparation: 15–20 minutes
Observation: 4–8 weeks
Investigation: 30–40 minutes

Skills tested: 5, 6, 7, 12, 13, 14, 15, 16, 23.

Materials

Preparation

- Leaves of oak or beech
- Twenty-five pins
- No 14 cork-borer (diameter = 2.0 cm)
- Marker cane

Investigation

- Record of results
- Graph paper

Instructions and notes

1 Pupils should select sites where leaf-discs are unlikely to be disturbed. Exposed positions on lawns, paths, etc. should be avoided.
2 The investigation may be carried out at any time of year. Even so, moist, green leaf-discs are eaten more readily than dry, brown ones. Results may be obtained more rapidly in the summer than at other times of year.

Answers

Part A   Marks

1 See Figure 47.   5
2 If leaf-discs had been pinned centrally, invertebrate animals may not have been able to remove them.   1
3 Wind. Rain. children, mammals or birds.   3
4 (a) Each leaf-disc has a diameter of 2.0 cm. The area of each disc ($\pi r^2 = 3.14 \times 1.0 \times 1.0 = 3.14$ cm. The area of 25 discs $= 3.14 \times 25 = 78.5$ cm.   3

(b) Take graph paper, graduated in mm². Draw 25 circles, each of 2.0 cm diameter. Place one disc on each circle, and trace around the edge of each leaf disc. Count, and then add together, the number of mm² units removed by feeding animals. Divide this number by 25. 3

Part B

5 (a) The marker can indicates where the bags have been buried. 1
 (b) The bag with 7 mm mesh, as it admits both invertebrates and saprophytes. 2
 (c) A sealed bag, without holes, containing 25 leaf-discs. 2

Fig. 47 *Fate of leaf discs over a period of 5 weeks*

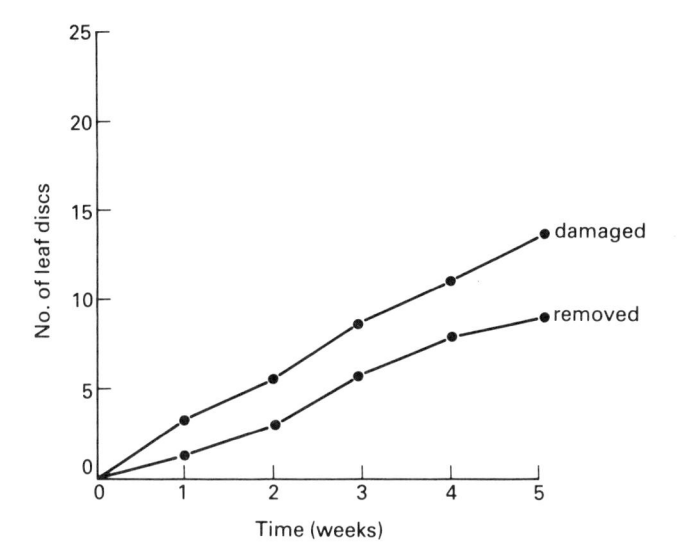

48 Gene recombination

TIME
Investigation: 30–40 minutes

Skills tested: 6, 7, 13, 16, 24.

Materials

- Four red marbles
- Three blue marbles
- Two teaspoons
- Two opaque paper cups, tins, or similar containers

Instructions and notes

1 Beads or aniseed balls may be used in place of marbles.
2 The sides of the containers used in this investigation should be opaque. Pupils should not look into the containers when removing marbles, or the recombination will not take place at random.

Answers

	Marks
1 (a) *AA*	1
(b) No. All are *AA*.	1
(c) Fertilisation.	1
(d) Each parent has itself received one gene from each of its parents.	1
2 (a) See Table 50.	1
(b) *Aa* and *aa*.	2
(c) 1*Aa* : 1 *aa*	2
(d) See Figure 48(i).	3
3 (a) See Table 51.	1
(b) *AA*, *Aa* and *aa*.	2
(c) 3*AA* : 9*Aa* : 4*aa*	2
(d) See Figure 49(ii).	3

Fig. 48 *Calculation of genotype ratio*

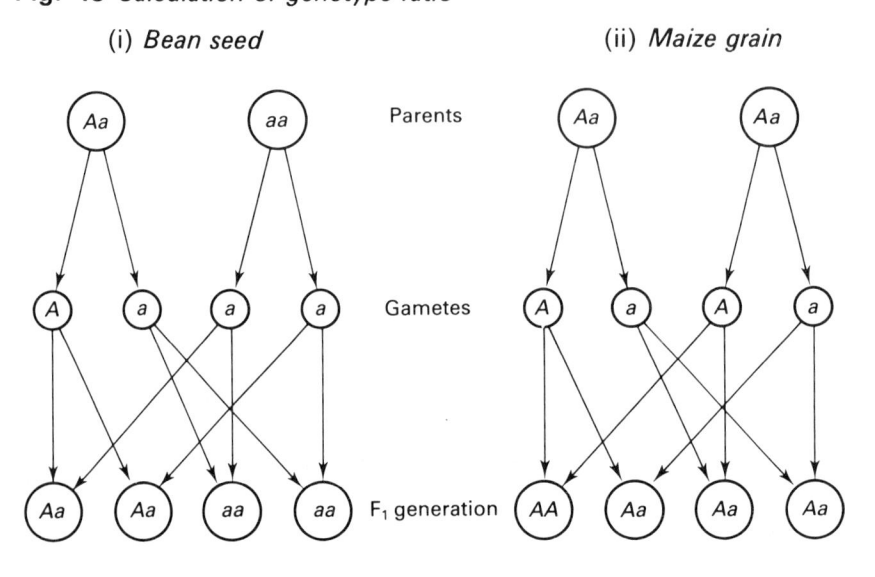

(i) *Bean seed*   (ii) *Maize grain*

Table 50 *Random matings between individuals of genotype Aa and aa.*

1 aa	2 Aa	3 Aa	4 aa
5 Aa	6 Aa	7 aa	8 Aa
9 aa	10 Aa	11 aa	12 Aa
13 aa	14 Aa	15 aa	16 aa

Table 51 *Random matings between individuals of genotype Aa and Aa*

1 aa	2 aa	3 AA	4 Aa
5 aA	6 aA	7 Aa	8 aA
9 aa	10 AA	11 AA	12 aA
13 Aa	14 aa	15 aA	16 aA

49 The sense of taste

TIME
Investigation: 30–40 minutes

Skills tested: 5, 6, 7, 13, 16, 18, 19.

Materials

- 2 cm³ sweet-tasting solution (A), in a flat-bottomed tube
- 2 cm³ salty-tasting solution (B), in a flat-bottomed tube
- 2 cm³ sour-tasting solution (C), in a flat-bottomed tube
- 2 cm³ bitter-tasting solution (D), in a flat-bottomed tube
- 1–2 g crushed onion, in a petri dish
- Five cotton buds
- Pocket mirror
- Glass or paper cup containing distilled water
- Paper cup

Instructions and notes

1 Solutions for tasting are prepared as follows:
Sweet-tasting (A): dissolve 2 g sucrose in 100 cm³ water.
Salty-tasting (B): dissolve 1 g sodium chloride in 100 cm³ water.
Sour-tasting (C): add 25 cm³ lemon juice to 75 cm³ water, or dissolve 5 g citric acid in 100 cm³ water.
Bitter-tasting (D): dissolve 0.5 g quinine sulphate in 100 cm³ water.
2 Use a kitchen liquidiser to grind fresh onions to a pulp with a little water. Each pupil will require 1–2 g crushed onion, supplied in a clean petri dish.

Answers

	Marks
2 See Table 52.	8

Table 52

Solution	Region of tongue			
	1	2	3	4
Sweet	✓	✗	✗	✗
Salty	✓	✓	✗	✓
Sour	✗	✗	✓	✗
Bitter	✗	✗	✗	✓

3 A sweet/salty taste in region 1, but no onion flavour.   2
4 (a) When the nose was not held, the onion flavour was very strong. This flavour masked the sweet/salty taste that was recorded when the nose was held.   2
  (b) The substance responsible for the onion flavour cannot be detected by the tongue, but is detected by the nose when minute quantities are inhaled.   3
5 If the mouth was not rinsed out after each test, some of the solution may have spread to other regions of the tongue. Distilled water was used because tap water may have contained some dissolved materials.   2
6 Apply in turn, to the region beneath the tongue cotton buds dipped into (a) sweet-tasting, (b) salty-tasting, (c) sour-tasting and (d) bitter-tasting solutions. Rinse out the mouth after each test. If none of these solutions are tasted, there are no taste buds beneath the tongue.   3

50 The skin as a sense organ

TIME
Investigation: 30–40 minutes

Skills tested: 5, 6, 9, 16, 18, 19.

Materials

- 5 cm^3 ethanol ■ Pencil ■ Dry cotton wool

Instructions and notes

1 Ethanol should be supplied in a stoppered container.

Answers

	Marks
1 (a) Tickling.	1
(b) Touch-receptor.	1
(c) Superficial.	1
(d) Front (ventral side) of arm. (Palm of the hand if the epidermis is thin.)	1
(e) Touch receptors are most numerous in the ventral side of the arm.	1
2 (a) Heat.	1
(b) Heat-receptors.	1
(c) Palm of hand.	1
3 (a) Cold.	1
(b) Cold-receptors.	1
(c) Palm of hand.	1
4 (a) Pain.	1
(b) Pressure-receptors.	1
(c) Deeper.	1
(d) Palm of hand.	1
5 Ask the subject to hold out their hand, palm upwards, and close their eyes. Apply the grid. Ask the subject to count the number of times their skin is pricked. Take a needle and lightly prick each square in turn. Score the number of needle pricks recorded by the subject out of 25.	5

Further reading

Alderson, P. and Rowland, M. (1985) *Biology for GCSE*. Macmillan, Basingstoke.
Andrew, B. L. (1969) *Experimental Physiology*. E. and S. Livingstone, London.
Bentley, G. I. (1981) *Microbiology: Technicians' Guide*. A. S. E., Hatfield.
Bishop, O. N. (1984) *Adventures with Microorganisms*. John Murray, London.
Bravery, H. E. (1976) *Home Booze*. Book Club Associates, London.
British Earthworm Technology Ltd. (1984) International Conference on Earthworms in Waste and Environmental Management: Abstracts.
Bunyan, P. T. (1985) *A Second Biology Course*. Stanley Thornes, Cheltenham.
Butler, C. G. (1974) *The World of the Honeybee*. 3rd edn. Collins, London.
Cerny, W. and Drchal, K. (1975) *A Field Guide in Colour to Birds*. Octopus Books, London.
Department of Education and Science, Welsh Office. *Science 5–16: a Statement of Policy*. H.M.S.O.
Edwards, C. A. and Lofty, J. R. (1972) *Biology of Earthworms*. Bookworm Publishing Co., Bungay, Suffolk.
Felix, J. and Hisek, K. (1983) *Garden and Field Birds*. Octopus Books. London.
Ferguson-Rees, J., Willis, I. and Sharrock, J. T. R. (1983) *The Shell Guide to Birds of Britain and Ireland*. Michael Joseph, London.
Freeland, P. W. (1973) Some applications of glucose-sensitive reagent strips in biology teaching. *School Science Review*, **55**, 190, 14–22.
Freeland, P. W. (1975) Some applications of agar-gel diffusion techniques. *School Science Review*, **56**, 195, 274–287.
Freeland, P. W. (1985) *Problems in Practical Advanced Level Biology*. Hodder and Stoughton, Sevenoaks.
Frisch, K. von (1967) *The Dance-Language and Orientation of Honey Bees*. The Belknap Press of Harvard University Press, Cambridge, Mass.
Fry, P. J. (1977) *Micro-organisms*. Schools Council, Hodder and Stoughton, Sevenoaks.
Hansell, M. H. and Aitken, J. J. (1977) *Experimental Animal Behaviour*. Blackie, London.
Mackean, D. G. (1983) *Experimental Work in Biology*. John Murray, London.
Mackean, D. G., Worsley, C. J. and Worsley, P. C. G. (1982) *Class Experiments in Biology*. John Murray, London.
McClintock, D. and Fitter, R. S. R. (1956). *A Pocket Guide to Wild Flowers*. Collins, London.
Peterson, R., Mountfort, G. and Hollom, P. A. D. (1954) *A Field Guide to the Birds of Britain and Europe*. Collins, London.
Phillips, R. (1977) *Wild Flowers of Britain*. Pan Books, London.
Richardson, D. H. S., Dowding, P. and Ni Lamhna, E. (1985) Monitoring air quality with leaf yeasts. *Journal of Biological Education*, **19**, 4, 299–304.
Scott, T. H. and Stokoe, W. J. (1936) *Wild Flowers of the Wayside and Woodland*. Warne, London.
Secondary Examinations Council in collaboration with the Open University (1986) *GCSE Science*.
Vere-Benson, S. (1960) *The Observer's Book of Birds*. Warne, London.

Index

Adventitious roots 55
Albustix reagent strips 7, 8
alcohol—see ethanol
algae 81
amylase 16, 17
apple 4, 5, 6, 22, 23
auxin 54, 59, 60
axillary bud 55, 63, 64

Bacteria 13, 16, 26, 27, 31, 76
banana 7, 8, 12, 14
barley grains 59
beans 9, 51, 60, 61, 62
beech 64, 82, 95
bees 43, 44, 45
bone 67, 68
brussels sprout 64, 65
busy lizzie 54

Canadian pondweed 38, 41, 42
capsule 48
carbon dioxide 9, 56, 71, 72, 73, 74, 75, 76
catalase 21, 89
cellulase 22
cellulose 23
cheese 7, 8
cherry laurel 32
chlorophyll 60
Clinistix reagent strips 4, 5, 7, 8, 30, 94
Clinitest tablets 4
cucumber 7, 8
currants 30, 31
cuttings 54

DCPIP tablets 8, 28
dicotyledons 46
diffusion 28, 30
duckweed 79, 80, 85, 86, 87

Enzymes 17, 19, 20, 25, 26, 40
epidermis 55, 56
ethanol 24, 25, 71, 74, 75, 101

Fermentation 73
fertiliser (artificial) 79, 80, 81
flora 78

flowers 43, 45, 46, 47
fructose 5
fungi 13, 14, 31, 52, 87

Genotypic ratios 98, 99
germination 51, 52, 53, 61
glucose 5, 6, 10, 11, 30, 31, 34, 35, 73, 74

Hazel 3
heart 70, 71
horse chestnut 1, 2, 3
hydrotaxis 66

Internode 55
invertase 4, 6, 95
ivy 82, 83

Lenticels 37
lime (*Tilia* sp.) 50, 64
Lincoln index 84
locust 1, 2

Maize grains 56, 57, 59, 60, 61, 62
maltose 5
mint 54, 55
monocotyledons 46

Nitrogen 93
node 55

Oak 64, 82, 83, 95
onion 4, 5, 6, 100
orange 12, 14
osmosis 34
oxygen 89

Peach 12
pear 1
pectin 23
pectolytic enzyme (pectinase) 22, 23
phosphorus 93
photosynthesis 38, 39, 40, 41, 42, 56, 60, 61
phototaxis 66
plantain 47
plumule 58
pollination 47

pollen 47
pollution 87
pond water 87, 88, 89
poppy 47
potato 4, 5, 6, 12, 14, 34, 35, 63, 64
polyanthus 45
protein 7
prunes 30, 31

Quadrat 49, 77, 78, 79

Radicle 58
raisins 7, 8
resazurin tablets 14, 16

Salt 10, 14, 32
seeds 48, 49, 50, 51, 52, 62
seed dispersal 47
seedlings 52, 53, 60
slug 52
slug pellets 83
snail 52, 84
soil 52, 91, 92, 94, 95, 96
stamens 47
starch 7, 8, 16, 24, 25, 30, 31

stigma 47
stomata 33, 37
sucrose 4, 5, 27, 75, 76, 94, 100
sultanas 7, 8, 30, 31
sugar 4, 5, 6, 7, 10, 26, 76
sycamore 47

Tooth decay 26
transect 49
transpiration 56
tropic response 59
trypsin 18
tulip 45, 46

Urea 92, 93
urease 92

Vitamin C 8, 9, 28, 29

Weedkiller 77, 78, 79
wilting 37
woodlouse 65, 66

Xylem vessels 37

Yeast 20, 21, 73, 74, 75, 85

Names and addresses of suppliers

B. D. H. Chemicals Ltd.,
Poole,
Dorset,
BH12 4NN

Griffin & George Ltd.,
Gerrard Biological Centre,
Worthing Road,
East Preston,
West Sussex.
BN16 1AS

Philip Harris Biological Ltd.,
Oldmixon,
Weston-Super-Mare,
Avon.
BS24 9BJ

Hughes and Hughes (Enzymes) Ltd.,
Elms Industrial Estate,
Church Road,
Harold Wood,
Romford,
RM3 0HR